HIT YOUR NUMBERS

&

KEEP YOUR JOB

A Practical Guide
to Major Account Sales Management

Scott Parker

i

DEDICATION

To my wife Kay, the love of my life.

TABLE OF CONTENTS

ACKNOWLEDGEMENTS

According to Ralph Marston "Excellence is not a skill, it's an attitude." In his drive for excellence, my mentor Doug McBurnie embodied that idea and encouraged me and many others to live our lives that way. He continues to inspire and I'll always be grateful our paths crossed.

Jo Major and Pat Edsell are men of like heart. Thanks to Jo for challenging me to take on this project and to both these men for their encouragement and incisive editing.

And finally thanks to all those I've worked alongside over the years whose ideas I've cribbed, made my own and included in this work.

"At the top of the mountain, we are all snow leopards."

Hunter S. Thompson

(July 18, 1937–February 20, 2005)

INTRODUCTION

At the beginning of my sales management career, it became clear that I had to balance two competing priorities.

First, I had to be in control of the numbers, both current revenues and the status of new business opportunities that my team was trying to close. Staying in control meant that surprises (particularly on the downside) had to be kept to a reasonable minimum. This was always important but particularly so in public companies, where management is measured on its ability to meet its published financial forecasts.

Second, I needed to make a personal impact in the field with customers by building relationships, closing business, and understanding market trends.

On top of these day-to-day priorities, I also needed to find time somewhere in the day to continue developing the selling strategy of the company.

And, we had to do this quarter after quarter after quarter . . .

Key Point: *Successful sales executives are able to balance two very different activities, effectiveness in the field and effectiveness managing the team and staying in control of the business.*

What was needed was a set of management processes that, with the least amount of effort, would provide adequate control of the business, thereby freeing as much time as possible to impact business in the field.

I looked for—but never found—anything published that helped build these processes, so I had to take what I could from others and make it up as I went along. I had the good fortune to have a few outstanding mentors and to work alongside a few other great sales managers. What I've learned I've essentially lifted from them. As Picasso said, good artists copy and great artists steal.

This book brings together what I've learned from others and crafted into a framework of management processes over the years. The material is presented as a practical guide, essentially a "how to" manual down to the level of providing templates and instructions for roll out.

Managing sales is a very different task depending on whether your customers are few or many and the product is a commodity or a highly technical product or service. The focus of this book will be on major-account selling, and specifically sales management, where it is critical to go a mile deep with a few customers rather than an inch wide and a mile deep with many.

Although the processes presented are the responsibility of the sales executive, they will be of use to major account sales people trying to improve their performance and certainly for those who aspire to sales management.

The tools in this book were developed in high-tech companies selling highly technical products, but the material is presented in a way that will be relevant to any selling situation where most of your revenue is tied up in a few customers.

To define our terms, a major account must represent a significant portion of a supplier's revenue (> 5% of revenue is a reasonable rule) whose product requirements have enough weight to impact your product-development plans.

Further, companies remain committed to resource and grow the relationship. There is cost and risk associated with bringing on new suppliers, so once you have developed a significant position, your major accounts have a real stake in your continued success.

Supporting customers of this size and importance will obviously affect how you resource them, the terms you'll agree to, and just about everything else. Within reasonable limits, you'll do whatever it takes to hold and grow market share.

As opposed to basing your selling strategy on a faceless set of demographics, a major account is better thought of as an interacting group of individuals who effect decisions with their own personalities, skills, and agendas. It is a family of sorts, with a distinct culture and style. As a result, a major account warrants a strategy customized to its specific opportunity and preferred way of engaging suppliers.

With respect to providing sales coverage, the term *penetrating* a major account is often used, and for good reason. Suppliers must develop deep relationships with their major accounts to increase the odds, even a few percent, of winning the big deals. You must assume your competition is building those bridges with important decision makers.

The relationship map between your company and each of your major accounts is complicated not only by the sheer number of people involved but because almost all functional groups in the "design, make, sell" chain of your company, including your executives, are touching these customers. The number and types of interactions on both the customer and supplier side make it an increasingly difficult environment to manage as the business grows.

Contrast penetrating a major account with providing account *coverage*, a term often used when discussing how best to cover the largest number of customers at the lowest cost. These smaller customers not only represent a smaller opportunity but are much simpler to interact with. The *milk run* is a term often used to describe the schedule a salesperson sets up to provide the needed coverage to their customers, either in person or over the phone/Internet.

Obviously, it takes a much more senior, experienced businessperson to develop and execute a major-account plan than it does to cover smaller accounts.

Key Point: *Managing major-account salespeople requires an approach very different from managing less senior sales people, affecting the metrics tracked, the sales skills you hire for and your management processes since you manage rather than supervise them.*

The purpose of the foregoing was to clearly bracket the unique characteristics of major-account selling and to highlight the rich and complex activity that must be managed to succeed with these most important customers. This book is devoted to improving your major-account selling program.

PROCESS MANAGEMENT VS. THE ART OF SALES MANAGEMENT

The successful major-account salesperson has a unique set of strengths. The skills required to build effective relationships, particularly with management on "both sides of the table," the ability to seize the moment in negotiations, the courage to overcome the constant stream of "no" and "that's not good enough" has to be embedded in the DNA of the salesperson.

It is a long list of skills, and although each can be observed and encouraged in the field, these skills can't really be taught; they must be hired.

Results, along with the selling processes that generate these results, can be measured and tracked with the same rigor as any other function in your company. A VP of sales I worked under years ago declared, "He who runs the processes, rules the world"—his way of saying that management processes set priorities, communicate progress to goals, and, as a result, create the culture of your sales organization.

Indeed, the sales function lends itself to management processes, as most of the success metrics (i.e., bookings, billings, etc.), as well as the management systems (goals and incentives), are measurable.

The best sales organization, and the one you should aspire to build, has the ability to hire the skills you can't teach and the business process discipline to track and drive to success.

GARBAGE IN, GARBAGE OUT

Good salespeople have good business sense and will support management processes provided they see value AND "the pain is worth the gain."

Too often this is not the case. Other functions (particularly marketing) too often request information from the field that isn't critical but soaks up precious selling time. The only way to manage this is to have all such requests approved by you, the sales executive. You're the only one in a position to decide if the request is worth taking away from precious selling minutes.

This is necessarily a defensive measure, but sales management must get involved in process design early and work carefully with other functions to design processes that meet the needs of all stakeholders with the highest level of efficiency. Remember, one of your roles, as the sales executive, is to be the guardian of the sales team's precious selling time with customers.

Key Point: *Required time to support management processes must be kept to an absolute minimum. Achieving this requires both saying no when needed to requests for information from other groups and designing efficient processes.*

Recall the priority of this book: to build processes that give you control over the business with the minimum time commitment required of you and your team. This requires that you be ruthless in your efficiency, both in the design and functioning of the measurement processes you roll out and in those imposed by other organizations.

THE JOURNEY AHEAD

We'll first review the scope of the sales function (chapter 2) and how to think through relationships between sales and other functions that touch the customer.

Chapters 3 and 4 present processes for managing and forecasting revenue, both from the current quarter and from a longer time horizon.

Chapters 5 and 6 focus on tools to close new business, including the substantial deals that can make or break your company.

Chapter 7 discusses strategy development, both for major accounts and for building a distribution strategy.

Chapter 8 covers the topic of incentive plans and how to make sure you get the most bang for your buck.

Chapter 9 presents how to organize resources to create the highest odds of winning "must win" opportunities.

Chapter 10 ties it all together by presenting a framework for including all of these processes into your busy week in a way that is manageable and consistent.

A FINAL POINT

John Stockton, whom many consider the best pure point guard to play basketball, was inducted into the NBA Hall of Fame by his Coach Jerry Sloan, a Hall of Famer himself (as player and coach). He capped his speech by saying, "John's great secret, the reason he was better than you, was that he worked harder than you did."

And so it is with major-account selling. The competition is so stiff for business at your major accounts, that your major-account managers must have great talent AND great work ethic.

The processes described in this book are all about bringing out the best in the significant investment your company makes in building a major-account selling team.

Every sales executive has areas in their program that need more work than others. To that end, each chapter stands on its own to allow the reader to move between topics (and chapters) as needed.

I'll close with a word of explanation on the rather cryptic Hunter Thompson quotation that opened this chapter. Snow leopards are considered by many as one of the most beautiful and rare animals. They can be found only above 11,000 feet in the rugged but beautiful mountain ranges of central Asia.

Rugged beauty, in the professional sense, surrounds those who have the courage to continue the struggle, day in and day out to hit their goals. The ability to bring two companies together (while working for one of them) and craft a win/win relationship in today's competitive markets is a beautiful thing to watch.

Here's to building an organization that performs at that level often enough to inspire you, help you keep your job, and prosper your company.

"I don't exactly know what I mean by that,
but I mean it."

J. D. Salinger, from *The Catcher in the Rye*

THE ROLE OF SALES

If you ask around a company regarding the sales team's responsibilities you will likely get different answers.

This kind of confusion creates opportunities for members of your sales team—like Salinger's Holden Caulfield—to be passionate and wrong. Chances are your customers see this confusion as well.

The first task in building an effective organization, and the topic of this chapter, is to ensure that everyone with customer-facing responsibility understands his or her responsibilities and deliverables and knows where to go to get things done.

FIRST . . . A REALITY CHECK

Although the role of sales will differ from company to company, one priority never changes and that it is the sales executive's responsibility first and foremost to know the revenue numbers and to be driving a plan to hit that quarter's revenue.

I recall meeting with the CEO on my first day as a new sales VP. After a few pleasantries, he shared his views on the strengths and weaknesses of my staff and his thoughts on what my priorities should be.

He closed our conversation by saying, "We've got a few weeks left in the quarter, and I'm concerned there are serious risks to the number we've committed to the board. By the day after tomorrow you need to come back to me with a high-confidence number and an action plan to close the gap to our target."

Welcome aboard . . .

The next 48 hours were a mad scramble to get our best grip on the numbers and a recovery plan.

The twin requirements, to know the numbers and to keep constant pressure on the team to hit the revenue target, shows up day one and forever defines a sales executive's responsibilities.

In the next chapter, I will present processes that will save you from the majority of these mad scrambles and give you control of revenue. You'll always be in a position to know the numbers, gaps, and actions required to close to target.

While staying on top of the numbers, however, you must build an organization that can drive the market opportunity in front of the company, and the first step is to make sure all team members are aligned.

When team members are aligned, efficiency increases, office politics decrease, and, above all, when people "say it like they mean it," odds are higher that they <u>know</u> what they mean.

Key Point: *A well-aligned organization will minimize the opportunity for people to speak passionately in favor of things they don't understand. A sign of a mature sales executive is that he or she balances the daily pressure to hit quarterly numbers while building a winning organization.*

ALIGNING THE ORGANIZATION

Just as the clutch in your car is the interface between the engine and the drive train, your sales team is the interface between your company and your customers. While the clutch delivers the power, it is also a central place for tension and heat.

To deliver power, the clutch plate needs to stay engaged and aligned with the drive train to operate properly. The clutch plate (your sales team) absorbs any misalignment, which causes chatter, heat, and wasted power.

The sales executive is responsible to ensure that the organization is aligned so that the customer views all interactions as clear and consistent. This is done by working with the executive team and by following these steps:

1. Get agreement on the need to define roles and deliverables. All functions that have regular customer interaction should participate.

2. Publish a schedule and include the template for distribution to their teams as shown in Figure 1.

   a. Include a due date for the completed deliverables matrix and a date for a team review.

   b. Note that there can be only one owner for a particular deliverable but more than one function can be listed in the supporting role.

Function (Ex. Applications)		
Deliverable	Owner	Support
Product Roadmap	Product Marketing	Applications

Figure 2.1.Template for Listing Deliverables by Function

3. After the templates are completed, hold a review with the relevant executives, managers, and team members. At this meeting each group presents their completed deliverables matrix by job function clarifying the working level

assignments; for example, which marketing person will support which salesperson.

Problem escalation should be discussed and agreed upon. The default escalation path is to simply bump these up the chain of command until the issue is prioritized and resolved.

For certain issues however, like field-product problems or issues with certain customers, it is better to short-circuit the chain of command and branch all problems to a specific manager. Most importantly, these procedures must be discussed and agreed upon between team members.

This type of review can be a great forum for group members to ask clarifying questions, articulate what they expect from supporting groups, and come away with a better sense of team cohesiveness. It is time well spent and can be combined with product training or other corporate planning to leverage the cost.

The output from this meeting should be posted on the company's intranet for reference and should be updated as needed.

DEFINING SPECIFIC ROLES

Let's use a concrete example to illustrate the process. Assume a portfolio of high-technology hardware components that customers incorporate into finished systems. We will map the responsibilities of those functional groups with substantial customer-facing responsibilities: marketing, customer service, applications, and sales.

For the following discussion, we'll assume that the executive team has met, agreed on the need for team alignment, and that the matrixes just discussed have been completed.

For each functional group we will review the responsibility matrix with relevant commentary.

SALES

In addition to these specific deliverables, the salesperson is the customer's "one neck to grab" for any problem

Sales		
Deliverable	Owner	Support
Deliver target for Bookings, Design Wins	Sales	Product Management
Deliver Revenue to target	Product Management	Sales
Lead negotiations (preparation & closure)	Sales	Product Management
Demand, Booking and Design Win Forecasts	Sales	Product Management
Leads Customer Strategy Development	Sales	Marketing
Owns resolving/elevating critical issues	Sales	

Figure 2.1. The Sales-Teams Deliverables

In this example, with respect to internal forecasts, sales "owns" the demand forecast and customer marketing "owns" the revenue forecast; the difference is that the demand forecast represents unconstrained demand (shipments assuming no constraints), and the revenue forecast represents the revenue the marketing team has judged to be committed to the company.

Beyond these hard deliverables, sales is responsible to sustain two aspects of the company's culture: ensuring a win/win relationship with the customer and ensuring that the company presents a clear and consistent face to the customer.

These two topics are important to discuss and resolve as a team.

Boiled down, sales is accountable for growing revenue to target and ensuring that a win/win relationship is maintained with the customer. This is crucial given that win/win relationships are the only way to generate long-term, profitable business.

Win/win does not mean that both sides are always happy with the outcome of a negotiation, but it does mean that both sides can live with the outcome of any single negotiation when put in the overall context of the relationship.

Generating a win/win outcome is often a difficult thing to pull off when the sides view the outcome differently, which is often the case in customer/supplier relationships.

Key Point: *The salesperson is always in the mode of changing the expectations of at least one side to drive the conclusion to win/win and must be able to do this reliably (i.e., better than their competitors).*

Getting to win/win requires three attributes:

1. A Command of the Facts

    In a negotiation, "he with the most data wins." Buying a car these days has almost become a fair fight, due to the large amount of data concerning the actual values of new and used cars available on the Internet.

    Beyond being prepared with the relevant data, sales professionals also need to tailor their proposals effectively for different audiences. For example, a proposal to a general manager will likely need to address profitability, while a proposal to an engineering manager may need to emphasize application support.

2. *Credibility*

A few years ago, my company released a defective product to a major customer that resulted in a field recall; a real disaster. The customer's divisional general manager lost his job as a result and, not surprisingly, we were approached for substantial damages.

Negotiations stalled as weeks quickly turned to months. Finally both sides agreed to mediation, given that neither wanted the cost and distraction of litigation.

Enter the judge.

The process was simple. Initially the judge met with each team, making it clear he wasn't ruling in the case but that he had ruled in many similar cases. After listening to both sides, he returned to each team and painted a bleak picture of the what could be expected if that team chose to allow the situation to go to litigation..,

Both sides (knowing that the judge was working each of us to the middle) had a simple decision: either trust the judgment of the judge or take our chances in court.

Predictably, we settled. What had been stalled for more than six months was completed in less than four hours.

Unlike the judge, sales professionals aren't neutral mediators in customer negotiations. Both customer and supplier know where the salesperson allegiance lay, but they do play a key role in calibrating expectations on both sides.

Key Point: *Personal credibility and integrity are key tools in any negotiation. Lose them and you've lost the ability to do your job.*

3. Closure as an Imperative

    Both sides in a negotiation need to want the deal to end with a win/win result.

    During that process there will be times when someone loses interest or is completely frustrated. At these times, sales professionals have to keep everyone at the table and working toward a resolution.

SALES AS CONDUCTOR

A sales professional can be viewed as a conductor of an orchestra. A conductor isn't there because he can play an instrument or compose the music. Rather, at show time everyone looks to the conductor to queue them, set the tempo, and make many musicians sound like one.

In much the same way, sales is responsible to ensure that the myriad interactions customers have with the company are consistent and unified in policy and approach.

The customer-facing part of the organization must understand that sales own this responsibility. To that end, sales is copied on all customer communications and should schedule, guide preparation for, and attend customer meetings. Sensitive business-development meetings with a customer are an exception; but even in these cases, sales should be aware of the meeting and updated on any items relevant to the current business.

For companies with a diverse product portfolio, marketing represents a broad array of both tactical and strategic activities. In my example, I will refer to "tactical marketing" as product management and "strategic marketing," including the profit and loss responsibility, as product marketing. Split this way, the product marketing team can focus on planning and execution with a limited number of distractions. Without this separation, the "crisis of the day" will continually swamp the calendars of those with the charter for strategy, and the company's future will suffer for it.

It is also easier and less costly to staff appropriately. Given the mix of technical and general management skills required, the product marketing function is the most difficult position to fill. It is frankly a waste to use these precious skills on tactical activities that could be done by a less-expensive and more broadly available set of skills.

Example deliverables for both product management and product marketing are presented below:

Product Management		
Deliverable	Owner	Support
Price Management-Deliver GM to target		
Product Training to the Field	Product Management	Product Marketing
New Product launch execution	Product Management	Product Marketing
Deliver Revenue to target	Product Management	Sales
Deliver target for Bookings, Design Wins	Sales	Product Management
Lead negotiations (preparation & closure)	Sales	Product Management
Demand, Booking and Design Win Forecasts	Sales	Product Management
Owns resolving/elevating critical issues	Sales	Product Management

Figure 2.2. Product-Management Deliverables

Product Marketing		
Deliverable	Owner	Support
Marketing P&L-Revenue to Gross Margin	Product Marketing	Product Management
Product Roadmap	Product Marketing	Product Management
New Product Development process	Product Marketing	Engineering
New Product launch execution	Product Management	Product Marketing
Owns resolving/elevating critical issues	Sales	Product Marketing

Figure 2.3. Product-Marketing Deliverables

In this example, product marketing is the owner of the marketing P&L (revenue through gross margin) and ownership of all aspects of the product portfolio. Product management becomes the execution arm (through sales) for product marketing. Given their P&L and portfolio responsibilities, it is no wonder that product marketing managers are often obvious candidates for general management positions.

To summarize, sales represents the "one neck to grab" for the customer, product management is responsible to product marketing (for execution) and product marketing to general management for hitting revenue/gross margin targets and driving the product roadmap.

Note that product marketing, not the sales team, owns the marketing P&L and therefore is the ultimate owner of revenue. This in no way lets sales (or product management) off the hook for delivering revenue, as they are responsible to product marketing to hit the number.

Slicing accountability from a different direction, sales must be the worldwide expert on their assigned customers in terms of strategy, what products they buy, and how products are purchased. Marketing must become the worldwide expert for their assigned product category by understanding technology trends, competitive product positions, and pricing models.

Key Point: *Given that both sales and marketing are active with customers and feel ownership for those relationships, particular care must be taken to make sure that these teams are aligned in heart and mind.*

Poor alignment causes problems. For example, marketing staff that meet with customers without informing sales occurs too frequently and leads to confusion with the customer and mistrust with the sales team. On the other hand, I've had to remind salespeople that they could only provide marketing-approved pricing and that the only company document they could sign was their paycheck.

The process I've detailed will align the hearts and minds of most, but sales management needs to immediately point out and aggressively correct any alignment problems should they arise.

CUSTOMER SERVICE

Customer Service		
Deliverable	Owner	Support
Order Mgt (Booking, returns, reschedules, etc.)	Customer Service	Operations
Resolve/Escalate logistics, order mgt issues	Customer Service	Sales
Deliver Target for Bookings	Sales	Customer Service
Service Metrics-Creation & Presentation	Customer Service	Operations

Figure 2.4. Customer-Service Deliverables

Once an order is booked, customer service owns that order and its management through shipment, including any required product returns. Customer service is responsible for ensuring that problems are resolved or escalated until resolved.

In addition, customer service will need tool support from IT to provide services, such as pre-expediting customer backlog (i.e., working and communicating delivery issues before shipment due dates) and identifying gaps in customer backlog relative to product lead times.

Customer service should also take responsibility for the quality of the customer's experience by organizing service metrics and making them available or, better yet, presenting them at business reviews with the customer.

Defined this way, customer service takes ownership of an important part of the customer's experience with the company, which is why sales and customer service develop a "hand in glove" relationship.

As a senior sales director with a large semiconductor manufacturer, I had the pleasure of working with someone who, for me, has become the gold standard for a customer service rep (CSR). Her name was Pat and she managed the CSR team for Hewlett Packard. Pat took personal responsibility to make sure delivery issues were elevated quickly and stayed on boil until solved. She was quick to call me or any other manager to get the problem fixed.

She also drove the customer to maintain the right backlog position and was tough but fair negotiating product-return issues. Pat really shined at quarterly business reviews as she presented the service metrics (pre-scrubbed with the customer of course) and as she drove both sides for improvement.

Pat would do anything legal and ethical to solve a customer's problem. I remember getting a call from Pat on Christmas Eve indicating that a Hewlett Packard location in Asia needed a shipping number to track a critical delivery to arrive on Christmas Day. Fortunately I had the home phone number of our operations director and soon after, we had the tracking number and a happy customer.

Pat was much more than a logistical administrator; she was viewed by the customer and by sales as a senior member of the account team.

Applications		
Deliverable	Owner	Support
Deliver to target for Design Wins	Sales	Applications
First order failure analysis-Resolve or escalate	Applications	Engineering
Product Roadmap	Product Marketing	Applications
New Product Development Process	Product Marketing	Applications

Figure 2.5. Applications Deliverables

Applications engineers (apps engineers) are a rare breed, requiring both good technical skills and good interpersonal skills to position them to ask the right questions, develop empathy, and thereby build effective relationships.

They support the design win process under the direction of sales, act as the first line of defense resolving customer development or manufacturing issues, and act as technical eyes and ears inside the customer organization for the marketing team.

Given their technical background and the lack of a sales title, apps engineers are able to build a more trusting relationship with customer engineers, which can be extremely useful when gathering competitive information.

Some years ago, my team was closing a networking IC design win with the largest network-adapter card manufacturer at the time. Whether we had to move slightly on the price of our IC to win (a few pennies on a few million units was a big deal) was a function of whether our competitor really had a qualified device available.

This information was, of course, not forthcoming from normal customer channels, so I pulled our apps engineer Mike aside. He had great relationships in engineering, and I told him that he needed to run this down for us.

Mike descended into the bowels of the customer's engineering organization, held discussions only he could have had, and returned with information that allowed us to hold our price, thereby earning his salary that year many times over.

Deciding how to organize applications—whether by product or geography and where they should report—is a topic unto itself, which we will leave for a later chapter.

I'll close with the thought that most companies start with product-oriented applications engineers (not generalists) reporting into the product lines and move to a field-applications model that reports to sales as the business scales, thereby driving a better cost of sales and getting resources closer to the customer.

PULLING IT ALL TOGETHER

Following the steps outlined in this chapter will ensure that each team member understands his or her responsibilities and where to get the support needed to do his or her job. The process will also foster a sense of teamwork as everyone becomes aligned.

There are many ways to organize around deliverables and the preceding is just one example. Scale, size of the customer base, and management discretion may lead to a different approach. The key is that everyone understands how it is done in his or her organization and what the deliverables are in that context.

I began this chapter by recognizing that understanding the current state of revenues is job one for a sales executive. This is simply a fact, but it is also true that he or she must at the same time build an organization that naturally delivers revenue to target and is a competitive advantage for the company. Getting alignment is the first step in building that organization.

After getting the team aligned with clear roles and responsibilities, a new sales executive then needs to implement an ongoing process that gathers information from customers, aggregates it, and crisply provides bookings and revenue forecasts to the corporation. This process, coupled with clear responsibility, will keep the sales executive out of "crisis mode" when it comes to managing revenue .The next chapter is devoted to that task.

"Effective leadership is not about making speeches or being liked; leadership is defined by results not attributes."

Peter Drucker

(Nov. 19, 1909–Nov. 11, 2005)

DRIVING THE QUARTER

Revenue growth and gross margin percent are the two most important and emotionally engaging indicators of corporate health and the most important for the sales executive. If you can forecast well, hit your numbers, and grow revenue, life is good. If you can't, being a sales executive is not the career for you.

If you ever talk with a sales executive after a missed quarter, you'll hear a combination of reasons why the revenue for the quarter was below target. External factors related to demand or an inability to supply to demand are the culprits.

The purpose of this chapter is to provide a structured process for forecasting and driving revenue. Specifically, for the current period—usually a financial quarter—you'll understand the high probability revenue number in enough detail at that point in time to assign actions to close the target.

A lot rides on calling the current quarter accurately because the company's operations are resourced to that number. In addition, your commitments are represented to outside stakeholders, such as your board and the investment community.

In a business with a large number of customers, where no one customer represents more than 1 to 2 percent of revenue, the customer changes throughout the quarter usually "wash each other out"; that is, they often don't move the overall revenue number. But when dealing with major accounts, where revenue is tied up in a few customers, one phone call cancelling backlog can tank your quarter.

When your overall market slumps, you'll get several of these calls, and revenue will go into free fall. All-hands conference calls will be launched, planes and trains will be boarded to beg for business culminating in a white-knuckle ride to close out the quarter.

Conversely, when an industry is red hot, you'll be scrambling to meet the needs of the customer. Companies that can best execute in uncertainty will gain share and increase profitability. Whether your company gains or loses in turbulent times, the responsibility to organize and mobilize the company for results will fall upon your shoulders as the sales executive.

With the process presented below, you will stay in control, because you will always have a high-confidence view of revenue and be driving actions to achieve the target.

This process requires that all the key stakeholders (sales, marketing and operations) understand their current quarter business at a very detailed (usually line item) level. There is just no other way to do it.

It is a big effort initially, but once everyone is on top of his or her business, you only have to manage the changes to remain in control.

In our example we will assume a portfolio of products managed by multiple marketing staff, a sales team serving a number of customers, and an operations group delivering the products.

Key Point: *Managing revenue to expectations is critical to the company and the single most important thing a sales executive does.*

The process centers around creation and judgment of the revenue file, which builds a current picture of revenue vertically by line item and horizontally by breaking the total for each line item into its elements of shipments, backlog, forecast bookings, etc. (see Figure 1).

The revenue file is at the center of a review meeting. The meeting is attended by all who have information needed to build a high-confidence view of revenue and of actions needed to close gaps to the revenue target.

The meeting is chaired by a member of the executive team (you as the sales executive are an excellent candidate), who asks hard questions and generates the "positive tension" to bring out the best in the team. The process owner actively moderates the meeting, with each product line discussion being led by the marketing team member for that product line.

Key Point: *A successful implementation of this process requires personal commitment from both the sales executive and the assigned senior resource to own and drive the program.*

Team members leave the review meeting aligned on the numbers and any actions they have to close prior to the next review meeting.

Management can learn a lot by watching the team in action. It is an opportunity to teach members of the marketing team how to organize across functional boundaries and drive the group. It provides a great insight into how effective sales and operations are at adapting to business conditions to produce maximum results.

In a fast-paced business with short product lead-times—that is, most technology companies—a weekly review cycle is appropriate. More stable businesses may be comfortable on a bi-weekly cycle, moving to weekly reviews in the last month of the quarter.

A process owner must be assigned the task of preparing the baseline numbers, actively moderating the review meeting, and publishing an updated file with action items resulting from the meeting.

I've used the term *actively moderating* because the role requires more than just seeing that these particular trains run on time. In addition, the process owner must jealously safeguard the integrity of the process and challenge the team to deliver a good product.

So, beyond having excellent data-management capability and good project-management skills, the process owner needs to be tenacious, have a thick skin, and possess a healthy sense of humor. Exceptional energy and courage are also required to drive this process, which can feel like "herding cats" even on a good day.

Likely candidates for the position of process owner are the leader of sales operations or a senior member of the finance team. Give careful consideration to the candidates for this job, as the person who fills it will make a significant difference in the quality of the process.

This position provides a great learning experience and career growth opportunity because the process owner learns how the various functions of the business interact in the entire book-to-build-to-ship-to-bill process.

The workload for the process owner can range from two days a week to a full-time job, depending on the size of the portfolio.

Key Point: *Assigning a process owner is a "critical hire" requiring a wide range of skills, a lot of energy, and a big dose of courage.*

PREPARATION OF THE REVENUE FILE

The process revolves around the revenue file, which details the current status of revenue relative to target. A general version of the template is shown below in Figure 1.

Figure 1 is a basic view, breaking out shipments, backlog, and "turns" bookings. If there are other significant sources of revenue, such as strategic inventory programs or unscheduled backlog, additional columns must be added to complete the picture.

Key Point: *Building the correct revenue template for your business is a matter of starting with shipments and, moving left to right, thinking through all the additional components that complete the view of revenue.*

Customer	Prod Family	SHIP$	$ Comm Backlog	$ Comm Rev	$ At Risk Rev	$ FCST	$ Unbkd FCST	BKNG/SH P	Mktg Adj. FCST $	Upside to Total $	TOTAL PERIOD	Upsd $	Opty $	Action	Owner
		A	C	D	E	F	G	H	I	J	K	L	M	N	O	P
Cust A	Prod Name	$ 2,000	$ 1,200	$ 3,200	$ 100	$ 4,000	$ 900	80%	$ 3,820	$ 200	$ 4,020	$ 300	$ 4,320	Book Order	John D
Cust B	Prod Name	$ 1,000	$ 600	$ 1,600	$ -	$ 2,500	$ 900	64%	$ 2,230	$ -	$ 2,230	$ -	$ 2,230		
Cust C	Prod Name	$ 1,500	$ 1,300	$ 2,800	$ 50	$ 3,500	$ 750	80%	$ 3,450	$ 100	$ 3,550	$ 100	$ 3,650	Qual	Mary W
Pline A Total		$ 4,500	$ 3,100	$ 7,600	$ 150	$ 10,000	$2,550		$ 9,500	$ 300	$ 9,800	$ 400	$ 10,200		
Cust D	Prod Name	$ 4,000	$ 2,400	$ 6,400	$ 100	$ 8,000	$3,400	80%	$ 9,020	$ 200	$ 9,220	$ 300	$ 9,520	Book Order	John D
Cust E	Prod Name	$ 1,000	$ 600	$ 1,600	$ -	$ 2,500	$ 900	64%	$ 2,230	$ -	$ 2,230	$ -	$ 2,230		
Cust F	Prod Name	$ 3,000	$ 2,600	$ 5,600	$ 50	$ 7,000	$2,900	80%	$ 8,160	$ 100	$ 8,260	$ 100	$ 8,360	Qual	Mary W
Pline B Total		$ 8,000	$ 5,600	$13,600	$ 150	$ 17,500	$7,200		$ 19,410	$ 300	$ 19,710	$ 400	$ 20,110		
Family Total		$12,500	$ 8,700	$21,200	$ 300	$ 27,500	$9,750		$ 28,910	$ 600	$ 29,510	$ 800	$ 30,310		

Figure 3.1. Example of how to build revenue from its components, moving from right to left.

You'll recall from the previous chapter that our example company recognized the marketing function as the owner of revenue, so consistent with that, worksheets in this process are organized by product rather than by customer. The yellow columns contain baseline values inserted by the process owner during preparation, such as shipments to date, and calculated values, such as total quarter view. The columns in green are those judged by marketing, and the columns in blue are updated by sales for review during the call.

The definitions of each column are on the next page.

Column Definitions

A. Customer name.

B. Product name: Note that the column header is named *Product Family*. Based on how the company views the portfolio, each worksheet could represent a product line or a product family made up of a few product lines.

C. Shipments to date.

D. Backlog committed to ship by operations.

E. Sum of columns C and D equaling committed revenue, meaning the business is either shipped, or booked, and operations has committed to ship.

F. Committed revenue currently viewed as "at risk." Examples could be breaking news on a production problem or a demand issue. How much revenue to consider "at risk" is a judgment call.

Throughout this chapter, any number that involves judgment will be called "judged." Care should be taken to always clarify which person or function is making that judgment. In this example, the "at risk" revenue for a product line is judged by marketing.

G. Total revenue forecast for the quarter taken from the company's current forecast.

H. Turns revenue; that is, revenue that must still be booked **and** shipped or "turned" in the quarter. This is calculated by subtracting committed revenue (F) from total forecast (G).

I. Probability of booking and shipping or "turning" in the quarter. Percentage judged by marketing.

J. Marketing adjusted forecast. This is the number that marketing feels is an accurate view today, assuming team members follow through on currently identified actions.

The value is a calculation of committed revenue (E) minus revenue at risk (F) plus remaining bookings forecasted to "turn" in the quarter. "Turns" bookings are calculated by multiplying unbooked forecast (H) by probability of booking/shipping (I).

K. Upside to total dollars. If the team finds additional high confidence revenue between the time the file is distributed to marketing for review and the end of the review meeting, those dollars are included here. These are usually additional "turns" bookings. This number is judged by marketing.

L. Total quarter revenue. This is the best prediction from marketing of where the quarter will close for that line item. It is a calculation of committed revenue (E) minus "at risk" revenue (F) and any expected turns bookings (calculated by column I plus any upsides in column).

M. Potential upsides. Any additional upsides captured by the sales team. If these are judged by marketing to be solid enough to add to total quarter revenue, these dollars will move to upsides (J) or be seen as an increased "turns" booking probability (I).

N. Possible revenue. Total possible revenue as calculated by summing columns L and M.

O. Actions needed to drive possible revenue (N). Captured by the process owner during the review meeting.

P. Name of action item owner.

PREPARATION FOR THE REVIEW MEETING

Initially, the process owner loads fresh shipments/backlog data from the system (yellow columns) into the worksheets. Marketing adjustments and sales inputs from the previous cycle are preserved, which will calculate new values for total quarter revenue (L) and possible revenue (N). The process owner then publishes the file to marketing for review.

Marketing, in collaboration with sales and operations, reviews the file and judges all columns identified with green headings in Figure 1. Marketing team members submit their judged files back to the process owner for consolidation and distribution.

Figure 2 shows a suggested timeline for preparing the file, assuming a weekly cycle in working days.

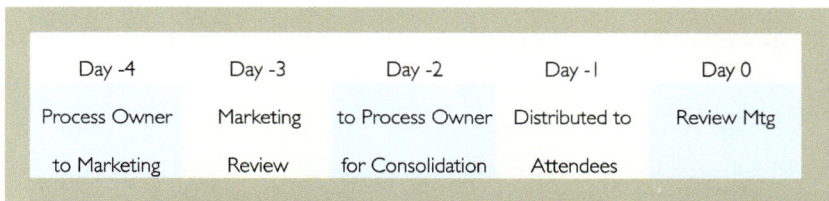

Day -4	Day -3	Day -2	Day -1	Day 0
Process Owner	Marketing	to Process Owner	Distributed to	Review Mtg
to Marketing	Review	for Consolidation	Attendees	

Figure 3.2. Suggested timeline for a review cycle starting with the revenue file going to marketing for review and completing with the review meeting

These are tight timelines, but keeping the cycle compressed ensures that the team is working with fresh baseline data.

The process owner, with the support of the entire executive staff, should require that deadlines be respected. This is particularly important if there are multiple marketing team members judging the worksheets.

If a deadline for returning a judged file is missed, the tardy team member is working with old data, resulting in a largely pointless review meeting. Hold the team to the deadlines and make poor performance an uncomfortable experience, and the good performers won't miss a deadline more than once.

Key Point: *Holding the team to deadlines as you move through the cycle is critical to keeping the process crisp. You will be challenged early, so make sure to hold people accountable.*

PREPARING FOR THE REVIEW MEETING

All participants at the review meeting must give the revenue file a careful review prior to the call. The review meeting is a very fast-paced affair so you need to come prepared with concerns, disconnects, and opportunities that came to light during your preparation.

As an aid to everyone's preparation, the process owner can create summary worksheets (Excel Pivot Tables) from the revenue file. Examples include slicing totals by customer or by product line, building lists for required turns bookings, or sorting possible upsides from high to low.

My preference is to review the file by starting with the largest customers and identifying meaningful changes. The 80/20 rule comes into play in a big way. Review the changes, starting with your largest customers, and a simple story will jump out at you.

Be sure to think through how you want to review the data, and work with the process owner to incorporate summary worksheets to support preparation for the review meeting.

THE REVIEW MEETING

The process owner moderates the meeting. Communication ports are opened and the meeting begins on time.

To give context, the process owner provides an overview of significant issues observed since the last review meeting. The moderator then rotates through each marketing team member to review his or her product line(s). For the sake of efficiency, a formal rotation can be established so that each marketing team member joins the meeting around the expected time to review his or her business.

Opportunities for upsides should be explored. Disconnects are resolved and any changes to the numbers are captured by the process owner, along with relevant action items.

The flow of the discussion moves line item by line item, generally moving left to right along Figure 1 and stopping to discuss any number that requires action and commitment to close a gap or capture an upside.

There is not time to review every line item, and marketing team members should focus on those few larger line items that require action and represent a gap to target that needs to be closed or an upside that can be captured.

Ideally, the marketing, operations and sales teams are aligned on revenue at the end of the review meeting. If there are deadlocked items, marketing breaks ties during the meeting in terms of what is published. If needed, deadlocked items can be worked offline.

Any substantial changes from the previous week should be challenged to make sure they don't reflect panic on the downside or a lack of rigor in assumptions on the upside. Any late-breaking operations or demand issues need to be discussed and factored into the number.

Inventory available for sale should be highlighted and the sales team challenged to move it. Any possible opportunities are added to the possible upsides column (M). The sales team then takes responsibility to close the actions during the week so those dollars move into the upsides column (K) or, better yet, the backlog column (D) for the next review cycle.

Key Point: *The executive sponsor and process owner work together to keep the call moving forward, capturing actions rather than allowing discussion around details, and keeping the focus on the larger "80/20" line items.*

It is good practice to ask each member of the marketing team his or her view of "the range"; that is, the high, expected, and low numbers for that product line. Adding up these ranges at the end of the call is a useful benchmark to your gut feeling about the risk in the total quarter revenue number (L).

The length of the meeting depends on how many product lines need to be reviewed, but ideally the call runs for about an hour, perhaps a little longer. If substantially more time is required, consider breaking the review meeting into two calls.

You will likely find calls taking longer at the beginning of the quarter when the numbers carry more risk and the team is getting organized around them. The calls should tighten and take a little less time as you move toward quarter end.

After the call is closed, the process owner cleans up the numbers, documents action items generated during the call, and publishes a final file to all attendees.

When the call is managed properly, everyone comes away aligned on the number for the quarter with a range top and bottom. Each member also understands the action items he or she must close prior to the next review meeting to close on the target.

Key Point: *Given the tight cycle (usually weekly), it is important not only that the call is crisp and focused, but also that the process owner publishes the updated revenue file the same day.*

THE ART OF DRIVING THE REVIEW MEETING

Assuming the sales executive chairs the call, he or she plays the critical role of setting the tone and driving the meeting forward. The review meeting will set the standard for how you expect your team to drive themselves and the company.

Consider the following when preparing to run a meeting:

- Use the 80/20 rule. The only way to keep the call on track is to keep the discussion focused on high-value line items, particularly those that experienced change during the week.
- Estimates should always reflect what the person feels is most likely. It's the answer to the question, "If you had to put $1000

of your own money on this number, what number would you pick?"

- Avoid rat holes. Help the process owner keep the call moving forward. When the call dives into an issue, take an action and move on.
- Be aggressive, particularly when it comes to finding creative ways to make up gaps, move unsold inventory, and solve operations problems, etc. But do not force people to sign up to numbers or actions they don't believe in. It is much better to start with numbers/actions the team believes are reasonable, execute on those actions, and then work on the next set of actions to improve the revenue view.
- Identify poor preparation or a lack of urgency, and do it publicly.

In preparation for one particular review meeting, I noticed that our largest customer had dropped two of their high-volume line items by almost a third from the previous week, firmly placing the quarter into the disaster category.

During the review meeting someone mentioned almost casually that the reason for the decline was that the customer "didn't need it anymore." I had to single out that salesperson on the call and send them packing to build a recovery plan, which in this case required an emergency customer visit. The situation provided an opportunity to build a better plan and send a signal to the team that when they bring bad news, they must have the details and a recovery plan already set in motion.

Said another way, the tone of the review meeting needs to be characterized by "positive tension." Facts, ideas, and potential opportunities to improve the number need to be aggressively challenged but in a constructive way.

Keep the focus on problems and opportunities, not on the people. Issues with team members should be saved for face-to-face conversations at a later time.

Contribute. Make sure to personally bring ideas for additional upsides to the table. You're not there to keep score but to improve the plan and to challenge and commit the team.

Have a path to the target. Every call should end with a path to hitting the target. If the number has collapsed, it may be a high-risk plan. But there should still be opportunities in column M that can be worked to get back to the target. You need to set the expectation with the team members that they are never off the hook to hit the revenue target.

The test of whether an action item should be taken is whether it is a reasonable request from a business perspective, even if it is difficult or awkward to approach the customer.

For example, a customer may not be contractually required to take a particular shipment, but if the company can call in a "marker" from a past favor, then you should try to make it happen. Even if they don't agree to take the shipment, they'll owe you one next time.

If a member of your sales team gives you push back, the old adage "if the products sold themselves, the company wouldn't need us" is true and a good point to reinforce.

Key Point: *The key to a good revenue call is that everyone comes prepared knowing their business and bringing ideas on how to close any gaps to the revenue target.*

ISSUES TO WATCH

Given that this meeting centers on revenue—the beating heart of the business—it is crucial that this process is consistently effective, as it is your best option to keep the organization aligned and to knock down actions to hit the revenue target.

However, given its cross-functional nature and all the moving pieces, there is a lot that can go wrong. Below are issues that can render the process ineffective and put you at risk of losing a clear view of your revenue.

- Care should be taken in choosing the day for the review meeting. Friday and Monday are obvious choices. If the file goes out on a Friday, everyone can review it over the weekend and be prepared for Monday. On the other hand, Monday is typically a packed day for many companies, and having the meeting on Friday allows for a less-distracted and more-focused meeting.

- The VP of sales and the VP of operations should attend the review and be active in driving their teams. Other executives, particularly the CFO and CEO, are welcome to attend the meeting, but they should be careful not to disrupt the tenor and flow of the meeting.
- If a senior executive wants to weigh in during the call in a significant way, this should be coordinated with the process owner to make sure that the meeting stays on track.
- Challenge the team, work issues, and make people really focus on performance. Be relentless, but also be relentlessly fair. Being tough does not mean being senselessly brutal; you need people working creatively, not shutting down due to fear. "Facts are friendly" and remember to focus on the problems, not the people.
- Never override the number the team believes in; otherwise the numbers, *and the process itself,* lose all credibility. If the executive team wants to challenge the output of the review meeting, this is perfectly appropriate, but it should be done in a separate meeting.
- This process can scale from a startup to a Fortune 500 company. As the number of product lines and summary reports expand, Excel becomes an increasingly unwieldy platform. In this case, it is straightforward to migrate the process to a custom application bolted to the corporate MRP system.

You'll come up the learning curve a lot faster if you, as the sales executive, chair a meeting with the process owner and a few other team members from the early review meetings to generate lessons learned and drive improvement.

With this process running and modified to your needs, you will have an aligned team where everyone understands the current status of revenue and the actions required to close the gap between the current view of revenue and that quarter's target.

Once you have a firm grip on the current quarter, you'll need to shift to a longer forecast horizon, with very different objectives. It's to that task that we now turn.

"Victorious warriors win first and then go to war, while defeated warriors go to war first and then seek to win."

Sun Tzu, *The Art of War*

REVENUE FORECASTING

In the last chapter we reviewed a process to enable you to keep a firm grip on your current quarter revenue, emphasizing that if you can't manage the current quarter revenue to expectations, you won't have a career in sales management.

The ability to forecast revenue over time isn't quite as critical to your career as driving the current quarter, but it's awfully close.

This chapter will focus on forecasting revenue beyond the current quarter; more specifically, forecasting for the time frame that aligns with the planning horizon for your company.

A reasonably accurate revenue forecast is crucial to a company's survival. Many companies have been ruined because they put in substantial capacity as the market turned down, or they didn't increase capacity and missed a market upturn. As the sales executive, you, more than any other member of the executive team, will be held responsible for forecast accuracy.

Forecasts based on hope rather than fact can be devastating. Years ago, as a sales manager at National Semiconductor, I attended a management meeting where the founder and CEO, Charlie Sporck, informed us that we only had enough cash to run the company for eight more weeks. We had bled cash to this dangerous level as a result of too often sizing the company to forecasts that predicted growth, which never materialized. This cost Charlie his job. Shortly thereafter Gil Amelio, our new CEO, sized the company to realistic projections of revenue and literally saved the company.

Key Point: *The process to build the revenue plan is mission critical for your company. Even though you won't own this process, you will be responsible for its accuracy.*

In the opening quotation, Sun Tzu emphasizes the value of forecasting in a military context, stressing the importance of understanding the relative positions and strengths of both armies, which allows the general to judge what can be realistically accomplished. This same concept holds in business and particularly so in terms of forecasting revenue results.

This chapter will present a structured process that brings the sales and marketing teams together to build the most accurate forecast for that snapshot in time. The process creates a picture of the best- and worst-case scenario and a way to track actions to maximize results. A sample forecast cycle will also be reviewed as well as ideas around building a longer-range forecast.

After presenting concepts around revenue, the discussion will turn to forecasting bookings. Not many companies do a bookings forecast, but it is a great cross-check to the revenue forecast. It drives the team to develop an understanding of how the customer-order placement process works. It also keeps the team focused on generating bookings.

FORECAST PARAMETERS

Make sure there is alignment with all participants and users around the assumptions and parameters used in building and reviewing forecasts. Consider some of these key issues:

- Every number in the forecast should represent the "most likely view" and should answer the question, "if you had to put $1000 of your own money on a number, what number would you pick?".

- The corporate planning horizon should align with the revenue forecast; that is, if the company does a rolling 24-month financial plan, the revenue forecast should provide a 24-month rolling view.
  The same is true of frequency. If all of the planning

numbers are revised monthly, the forecast should be done from the ground up monthly as well and timed so that the forecast feeds directly into the rest of the planning process.

Since conditions can change quickly, a quarterly revenue forecast is not frequent enough for sales and marketing to stay in control of the business. So, for those companies on a quarterly planning cycle, doing a "light" forecast inside sales and marketing (only updating substantial changes) will keep the sales and marketing teams on top of their numbers.

- Ideally, the forecast will be at the line-item level, meaning a line item for each potential customer order. There is just no other way to generate a forecast that reflects an understanding of the business. If the business is made up of many small value transactions, then the only option is to forecast at the product-family level.

- Sales should generate a view of unconstrained demand, which is then realistically judged by marketing to create a revenue plan. For our purposes, "unconstrained demand" represents revenue that can be generated, assuming no technical or quality issues exist. It also assumes an unlimited supply of product from operations. Understanding this view defines the highest possible revenue number, where output is perfectly matched to demand.

Retaining both views captures maximum information from the process. The judged revenue plan generated by marketing becomes the key output of the forecast and feeds directly into the corporate planning process. This also allows the CEO and CFO to understand with good detail how the forecast is constructed and what risks it contains.

- Direction needs to be provided around which products should be forecasted. A reasonable rule in a technology business is to only forecast products that are in production or that have committed release dates from marketing. Bear in mind that marketing usually provides aggressive product-introduction dates.

  Another potential distortion in the numbers is reflected in the natural pressure from sales to lower the numbers to drive lower quotas and for marketing to drive the numbers higher in the outer quarters to secure more resources. These biases need to be considered when the executive team is reviewing and judging forecasts.

Key Point: *Marketing will want relatively high numbers in the forecast to increase investment dollars and sales will want lower numbers to encourage lower quotas. Operations will have its own view of forecasting, as will finance. These biases are a natural part of business life and need to be factored into your judgment of the numbers.*

THE FORECAST CYCLE

Proper implementation will require a consistent resource to organize the forecast, drive the process, and push for follow up. Depending on the size of the organization, this could mean anywhere from a few hours a week to a full-time job for more than one person. Given that this forecast drives everything from capital purchases to customer satisfaction, it's a highly leveraged investment, so make sure to resource appropriately. This chapter will refer to this resource as the process owner.

The general template for the revenue forecast is straightforward, usually with columns for the quarters being forecasted from left to right and rows provided for individual products. The initial working file is organized by customer, which makes it straightforward for sales to provide their input.

An example forecast cycle is provided below:

1. Prior to publishing the working file, you, as the sales executive, should set the tone for that forecast with the sales team by providing a view of overall market conditions. You should include your view of demand from your "customer's customer"; that is, one level up the value chain as well as any customer specific issues or particular market segments that you believe are seeing strength or weakness.

   This is also a good place to set expectations about new product availability, changes to pricing policies, or any other changes that could affect the forecast. Providing your baseline view is good practice, as the team will then judge their forecasts with an aligned view of the macro factors driving the forecast. The odds will be much better that the file that arrives for your final review will be consistent with your views.

2. After a working file has been published and each salesperson has provided their inputs, sales management is allowed a limited time frame to review the numbers with their teams. Following this review, the working files are returned to the process owner for consolidation according to schedule.

   To ensure there is alignment, the sales team should have a formal review meeting with the marketing team. A spirited challenge to the numbers will improve the quality of the forecast and the sales team and the marketing team will be much better informed as they judge their revenue plan.

   The sales executive should also do a final review of the forecast, which can be done in conjunction with the marketing review or separately. After the final review, the unconstrained view is "locked" and forwarded to marketing to be judged against operational, market, and new product risks.

3. The judged numbers are consolidated by the process owner and distributed to executive management for final approval, which then becomes the official revenue plan for the company.

An example timeline is presented below in Figure 1 (in working days).

Day -8	Day -7	Day-4	Day -2	Day -1	Day 0
Discuss	Data Set	Sales	Marketing	Executive	Locked
Trends	Distributed	Approval	Approval	Approval	Forecast

Figure 4.1. Sample Timeline for a Forecast Cycle.

Key Point: *Keep the forecast cycle as short as possible. The tension in a tight cycle is positive to the process, the organization will spend less time creating the forecast, and it will be available earlier in the period. A process that is short, but repeated often, will respond better and faster to changing demand.*

FORECAST REVIEW MEETINGS

In Figure 1 above, three working days are provided for sales to lock unconstrained demand, which is adequate for one level of sales management to review. This time frame can be modified to match any additional levels of review needed.

Sales owns the unconstrained number and hence makes the final call, but with marketing actively participating in the building of unconstrained demand, both sales and marketing should come away well aligned on the overall possibilities for revenue. Therefore less time is needed for marketing to lock the revenue plan (as noted in Figure 1).

As a rule, there should be few disconnects between the sales and marketing teams on their view of the forecast in the first two quarters. If there are substantial disconnects, there is a problem with your process or the quality of the effort. The sales team should have good visibility into the customer's view of their demand over the next quarter.

As the forecast moves beyond two quarters, tension in the views of the sales and marketing teams will likely appear. The marketing team usually takes a more aggressive view of revenue rolling in from the introduction of new products than the sales team.

Key Point: *Substantial disconnects between sales and marketing, particularly in the first two quarters, points to a problem either with the quality of the effort or the process.*

As the sales executive, you own the unconstrained demand number so you must make sure you're comfortable with the final product.

JUDGING FORECASTS

As noted earlier, there are many ways to organize the forecast template for your review. Figure 2 below provides a simple example.

Week:	3								
Customer	Product Family	Q-1 (Actuals)	Q 0 (FCST)	% Delta	% Firm	Q+1 (FCST)	Q+2 (FCST)	Q+3 (FCST)	Year Total
Cust A	Prod A SKU	2,000	2,400	20%	34%	2,600	2,400	2,600	10,000
Cust B	Prod A SKU	1,000	800	-20%	62%	900	1,100	1,300	4,100
Cust C	Prod A SKU	1,500	1,700	13%	75%	1,500	1,600	1,750	6,550
	Prod A Total	4,500	4,900	9%	53%	5,000	5,100	5,650	20,650
Cust A	Prod B SKU	4,000	3,400	-15%	27%	3,200	4,200	4,400	15,200
Cust B	Prod B SKU	1,000	1,100	10%	45%	1,300	1,400	1,350	5,150
Cust C	Prod B SKU	3,000	2,600	-13%	71%	2,800	3,600	3,700	12,700
	Prod B Total	8,000	7,100	-11%	46%	7,300	9,200	9,450	33,050
	All Products	12,500	12,000	-4%	49%	12,300	14,300	15,100	53,700

Figure 4.2. Sample Revenue Forecast Template. Discussion purposes around judging numbers.

In this example, the column titled "Q-1 (Actuals)" provides the previous quarter actual revenues. Columns titled "Q+1 (FCST)," "Q+2 (FCST)," and "Q+3 (FCST)" represent the succeeding three periods for comparison.

The column titled "% Delta" indicates the percentage change from Q-0 from Q-1. The column titled "% Firm" is a calculation of shipments to date for the current quarter plus backlog with current quarter ship dates indicating the percentage of the quarter's revenue that is in-house.

Comparing "% Firm" for the week you're reviewing versus "% Firm" for the same week in previous quarters is a good indicator of the risk in your current quarter forecast. For example, if a particular product family is historically 30 percent "firm" at the same point of the quarter and the file you're reviewing shows 40 percent "firm," the current quarter forecast could be conservative by up to 10 percent.

Key Point: *Comparing the "% Firm" for the comparable point in previous quarters is an excellent data point to judge risk in the current quarter forecast.*

You should also compare the changes in the forecast with your trends/market analysis prepared for the sales team at the beginning of the cycle. Netting these trends against the working file may yield disconnects that can be resolved in the review meeting.

When judging the forecast, you'll come away with a more thoughtful analysis and be able to present more information to the other executives if you create a high, low, and expected view of revenue with associated assumptions.

To generate a high/low range, review the forecast for those few high-value line items that could swing the number in either direction. Adding all of the potential increases generates the high end of the range, and the potential decreases creates the low end of the forecast. The key here is to focus on the high-value line items.

Key Point: *Generating a range (high and low) in addition to expected revenue is very helpful in providing color and assessing risk. In addition, the spreadsheet can be constructed to check for logical errors (high bookings, but low forecast, etc.).*

COMMON MISTAKES

As mentioned earlier, there is a natural tendency to bias forecasts to support the needs of the group generating the forecast, given the revenue plan is used for corporate planning.

I remember completing a forecast cycle during a very turbulent market period some years ago. That particular forecast was to be used as the baseline for our annual corporate plan.

I realized early that the group VP and I were rather far apart in our view of the forecast (he was higher than I was), which was unusual. The fact that this plan would be used to set quotas for my team and to allocate resources for his team surely biased both our views.

As a result, this became a particularly difficult forecast to resolve, ultimately requiring a presentation to the CEO to break the tie. We ended up with a better forecast, aligned across the team, because we were both required to defend our numbers in front of the CEO.

An even more common example, as noted at the beginning of this chapter, is to inflate the forecast beyond a reasonable expectation in the outer quarters to justify avoiding the bitter medicine that an honest forecast would dictate.

Entire industries, particularly those that don't yet have well-defined business models (think early Internet companies) or those that don't have clearly understood growth drivers (think start-ups) often have a tendency to overestimate long-range revenue forecasts.

Key Point: *Drive a culture that encourages participants to provide their honest view of the numbers by setting a good example in your personal forecast judgments.*

If you see a general drift up in the later quarters of your forecast, your team should be able to explain the increase in terms of new products kicking in, expected share gains, or an improvement in market conditions consistent with your trends analysis. If not, you're looking at unwarranted optimism, and those increases should be taken out.

There is a human tendency to assume the future will be like the present. This encourages us to underreact to signals that the market is changing. The result is that teams tend to be overly pessimistic for markets that are on the way up and too optimistic for markets on their way down.

This is a difficult issue to avoid and calls for you and your team to thoughtfully discuss any meaningful changes in metrics, such as booking and cancellation rates, to increase your chances of correctly predicting the slope of the revenue line. Certain metrics tend to lead others in time; for example, margin compression occurs before revenue falls, cancellations lead bookings, which leads revenue. Look very critically at changes in leading indicators; they are often your only defense against some very big mistakes.

You also have to remain vigilant to root out plain old sloppy thinking. Publishing forecast accuracy highlights patterns where accuracy needs to be improved. At a corporate level many of the misses will net themselves out, so you need to publish forecast accuracy on a fairly detailed level so that individuals within the organization can learn and be held accountable.

FORECASTING BOOKINGS

I remember the look on the faces of my team the first time I rolled out a process to forecast bookings. They thought it was the dumbest thing they had ever heard of and a complete waste of time.

It is true that we did struggle with it for a month or two, but we finally developed a useful process. Bookings are *THE* leading indicator of next quarter's revenue, so it was important to get control of these numbers.

Key Point: *A well-thought through bookings forecast is your best cross-check for next quarter's revenue forecast.*

Developing a bookings forecast will also drive your team to understand your customer's order-placement process. For example, does a customer's order-management system generate an order using only demand, inventory, and lead-time as variables? Or are there other risk issues that need to be considered in the equation?

A salesperson needs to have an understanding of the following to generate a bookings forecast: (1) how the customer's order process generates orders, (2) the current booking run rates, and (3) those few large-value line items expected to book.

Given the difficulty of predicting bookings and understanding that it is only used as a cross-check to revenue, the forecast should be generated at a relatively high level (such as at the customer level) rather than by line item.

Lastly, it is important to review revenue weekly, but I've found that reviewing the bookings forecast every other week is adequate given that, again, its primary purpose is to benchmark the revenue numbers. Figure 3 below presents an example bookings-forecast template.

Week	3				Q 0 Rev FCST	Rev FCST	Q0 BK 2 DATE	WK 2 BK	To Book	Q0 BK FCST	FCST Delta
Regions	Q-4 BK	Q-3 BK	Q-2 BK	Q-I BK							
Region 1	8,400	8,600	8,600	8,700	8,800	9,400	2,500	500	7,100	9,600	1,200
Region 2	2,400	2,700	3,300	3,400	3,200	3,600	1,400	800	4,300	5,700	(300)
Region 3	5,400	5,600	5,300	5,800	5,900	6,200	3,100	400	3,300	6,400	200
Region 4	3,700	3,800	3,600	3,800	3,700	4,200	1,500	100	1,500	3,000	-
Region 5	6,900	7,200	6,900	6,700	6,900	7,300	2,300	700	5,200	7,500	(400)
Region 6	1,900	2,000	2,000	2,200	2,100	2,600	800	200	1,600	2,400	-
WW Total	28,700	29,900	29,700	30,600	30,600	33,300	11,600	2,700	23,000	34,600	700

Figure 4.3. Example Bookings-Forecast Template—Summary Matrix.

Region 1	Q-I BK	Q 0 Rev FCST	Q +I Rev FCST	Q 0 BK 2 Date	WK 2 BK	To Book	M1 Booking	M2 Booking	M3 Booking	Q 0 BK FCST
Customer A	$ 2,200	$ 5,000	$ 5,600	$ 2,500	$ 500	$ 2,500	$ 1,000	$ 2,600	$ 1,400	$ 5,100
Customer B		$ 1,400	$ 1,500	$ 600		$ 1,300	$ 200	$ 700	$ 1,000	$ 1,900
Customer C	$ 200	$ 300	$ 600			$ 100			$ 100	$ 200
Customer D	$ 2,900									
Customer E	$ 3,200	$ 2,500	$ 2,100			$ 2,200	$ 200	$ 1,500	$ 500	$ 2,300
Region Total	$ 8,500	$ 9,200	$ 9,800	$ 3,100	$ 500	$ 6,100	$ 1,400	$ 4,800	$ 3,000	$ 9,500

Figure 4.4. Region-Level Detail of the Bookings-Forecast Template (Rolls up to Figure 3).

Figure 3 has two sections. The top is a summary showing region totals adding to a worldwide number. These numbers are calculated from the working numbers (by customer) in the lower section. Figure 3 shows the summary for one sales region (region 1) summarized from the detail in the lower section (Figure 4).

The columns titled "M1 Booking," "M2 Booking," and "M3 Booking" in the lower section (yellow) are the working cells where the sales team inserts its forecast for each month. These columns auto sum to the quarterly total (blue).

The columns to the left of the yellow columns provide the data required to judge the forecast. These include the previous quarters bookings (Q-1 BK), the current and next quarter revenue targets (Q 0 Rev and Q+1 Rev FCST), bookings so far in the quarter (Q 0 BK 2 Date), bookings for the previous week (WK 2 BK), and the delta between the total bookings forecast and bookings to date (To Book).

The cycle to produce the forecast is straightforward as it is generated and reviewed by the sales team. The process owner distributes the working file with updated actual bookings. The sales team updates the forecast (yellow columns) and returns it to the process owner who consolidates and publishes.

JUDGING THE BOOKINGS FORECAST

The bookings forecast is a good staff meeting agenda item. Staff meeting not only avoids putting another meeting on the calendar, it is also the right place to drive team members for additional bookings.

Reviewing the following points will prepare you for a discussion of the bookings forecast:

- Compare the bookings forecast (Q 0 BK FCST) with the next quarter revenue forecast (Q+1 Rev FCST). These numbers should be similar given the rule that you should book this quarter the value of what you ship next quarter (assuming no change in lead-times).

  Any meaningful delta between this quarter's bookings and next quarter's revenue forecast should be explained in terms of changing lead-times, new product revenue expected next quarter that has not yet booked, or one-time events like a last-time buy of a discontinued product or service.

If lead-times have extended, expect bookings to be larger than the next quarter revenue forecast. Obviously, the same is true in reverse; that is, if lead-times contract, bookings will also contract.

- Compare the forecast with the current quarter revenue forecast to determine if the book to bill ratio (bookings over billings) is consistent with what you would expect for this customer given current market conditions. If their business is strong, you should see a positive book to bill.

  Similarly, compare the forecast with the previous quarter's bookings to ensure the trend feels right.

- Lastly, compare last week's bookings (WK 2 BK) with what has booked so far in the quarter (Q 0 BK 2 Date) to confirm that the remaining dollars to book (To Book) can be achieved from a run-rate perspective.

I've used terms like *looks ok* and *feels right* to emphasize that judging a bookings forecast is not about the kind of accuracy you're driving for in a revenue forecast, but rather it is about making sure the assumptions underlying the numbers make sense and that bookings rates are on track. A large part of getting this right is looking at the numbers from the different logical viewpoints suggested.

KEY POINT: *A useful review of the bookings forecast looks at the relationship between bookings, which are the leading indicators of revenue, from several different points of view; for example, bookings versus next quarter revenue or bookings to date in the quarter versus the forecast.*

SUMMARY

The ability to generate and hit forecasts for the current quarter and beyond is critical for any corporation and the survival of any sales executive.

The key to building an accurate forecast is to do an adequate review of the business so you "know the numbers." This is accomplished by cross-checking them with as many data points as possible. This chapter reviewed many such relevant data points including a bookings forecast, the current backlog position, and a careful review of a forecast's slope to make sure the trend is justified.

Predicting future revenue is difficult, but it is definitely a skill that can be improved with effort using the concepts presented in this chapter.

This chapter, and the last, have discussed forecasting business for products that are already in production with customers. This is important to be sure, but the lifeblood of any company is closing new business opportunities.

Adding a process to forecast and to drive closure of new business to those from previous chapters will position you to project the company's revenue prospects as far as the product roadmap will take you. It is to that task that we now turn.

> *"If winning isn't everything, why do they keep score?"*

Vince Lombardi

(June 11, 1913–September 3, 1970)

CLOSING NEW BUSINESS

The last two chapters have focused on the topic of revenue forecasting, both driving in quarter results and generating a long-term forecast for planning purposes.

In addition to maximizing revenue for current products, winning new customer programs is critical for ongoing revenue growth and represents the lifeblood of any company. To that point, this chapter presents a process that the sales management team can leverage to ensure that their teams close the most important new business opportunities.

Key Point: *Closing new business is the lifeblood of any company. It is essential to sustain growth by replacing revenue from customer programs that are moving toward end of life.*

This chapter will use the term *design win programs*, or *design wins* for short, to refer to new business opportunities. It is the corporate responsibility of the sales and marketing team to generate design wins.

The 80/20 rule is more like the 90/10 rule when it comes to new business opportunities with major accounts. A very few programs have the potential to drive your revenue and market share past the competition. This fact underscores the importance of staying focused on these "must win" programs.

The process to maximize design wins has four objectives:

1. **Increase the odds of winning**. The process that customers go through to qualify vendor's products is very dynamic. To win business, your team

members must communicate on strategy, resourcing, and actions to close design wins in a timely manner. The process needs to provide a framework to document the strategy as well as track and drive the team's activity to successful closure.

2. **Prioritize resources**. Engaging with major customers on new business is a resource-intensive activity often requiring support across functional groups ranging from engineering to applications to quality. These scarce resources must be allocated thoughtfully to generate the highest return.

3. **Provide input to the revenue forecast**. Revenue from new products is an important factor when forecasting, even in the short term. Your methodology must provide a way of judging revenue from potential design wins into the overall revenue forecast.

4. **Keep focus on high potential opportunities.** Always remember that a strategy is only relevant to the snapshot in time in which it was created. As the customer moves toward a decision, a strategy must stay current to any competitive responses or changes in the customer's requirements. Given that your team is managing a number of potential design wins at any time, the process needs to naturally draw the attention of management to opportunities with the highest return.

The topic of building strategies for individual opportunities will be covered in a subsequent chapter. The purpose of this chapter is to provide a process that enables live-design win opportunities to be regularly reviewed for quality of strategy and execution and to allow the potential value of these opportunities to be properly reflected in the revenue forecast.

Key Point: *An effective methodology for driving design wins ensures that effective strategies are in place, resources are properly allocated and potential new business is accurately judged into the revenue forecast.*

The design-win funnel is an effective sales management concept that has been around for a very long time (see 1, below).

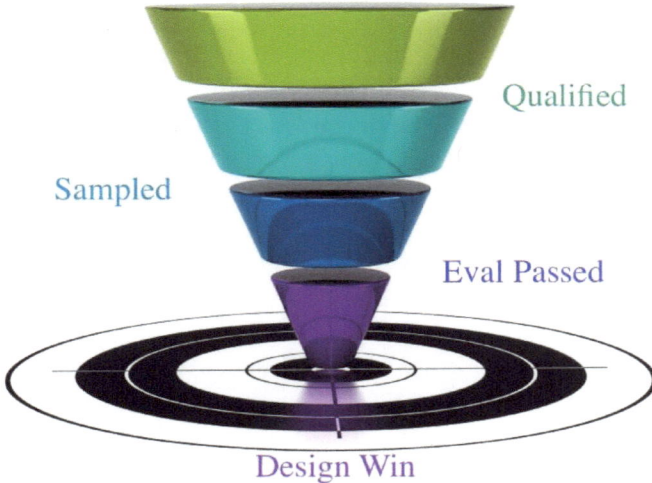

Figure 5.1. Funnel Graphic Illustrating the Flow of Opportunities Moving to Close

Initially, a large number of unqualified opportunities (above the funnel) are qualified by the salesperson. A qualified opportunity is one where a reasonably competitive product can be supplied at an acceptable price. Qualified opportunities then move through the selling process and either fall out the side of the funnel as losses or drop through the bottom as wins.

Figure 2 presents a simple design funnel using Excel. Column definitions are below.

Customer	Sales	Prod. Line	Product	Volume	ASP		Ext. Value	Total Value	Stage	Close	Actions
A	Person A	Line A	'Prod W	1000	$	100	$ 25,000	$ 100,000	2	12/10/11	Sampling
B	Person B	Line B	Prod X	1500	$	150	$ 33,750	$ 225,000	1	11/25/11	Presentation
C	Person A	Line A	Prod Y	800	$	75	$ 42,000	$ 60,000	3	1/10/12	Passed Eval
D	Person A	Line B	Prod Z	1200	$	50	$ 60,000	$ 60,000	4	10/10/11	Closed
					TOTAL		$160,750	$ 445,000			

Figure 5.2. Example of a Simple Design-Win Funnel using Excel

In Figure 2, each row represents a specific customer opportunity. Looking at the columns, **Total Value** captures the estimate of the opportunity's value for a specific time frame by multiplying the volume (for the first 18 months of production) and average selling price (ASP). For example, the total value of the opportunity with customer A is $100,000 calculated by multiplying 1000 units with the average selling price of $100.

The example uses 18 months as the time frame to calculate total value. Although this is a reasonable value for many high-tech products, other industries should consider a different metric. A good rule of thumb is to choose a time frame that captures something in the range of a third to a half of the average program life for your business.

The total value should represent your company's share of the volume, that is, your expected revenue, not the customer's total volume for the program. Using your current share for similar products is a good guideline for judging your likely share for new design wins. For products in new-product categories where you lack any history, your only choice is to use a reasoned estimate of share based upon your customer relationship.

The column titled **Stage** represents the position in the selling cycle for that opportunity. These stages will be different from industry to industry.

For our example, stages are defined as (1) opportunity qualified, (2) product samples delivered, (3) evaluation testing passed, and (4) design win or (5) design loss. These stages are appropriate for high-tech component or systems businesses. To define stages for your business, choose those concrete milestones that an opportunity will pass through on its way to closure. These milestones should also be useful markers for setting actions and goals.

Expected Value is a calculation of total value multiplied by a percentage weighting based on that opportunity's stage position in the selling process (as noted in the column titled **Stage**). The weighting percentage obviously will increase as opportunities pass more milestones on their way to becoming wins.

The example assumes that 15 percent of qualified opportunities, 25 percent of sampled opportunities and 70 percent of opportunities that have passed the customer's evaluation will eventually turn to design wins. The opportunity with customer A is in stage 2 so the total value is factored by 25 percent for an expected value of $25,000.

The total expected value for your design funnel can be a surprisingly accurate view of its value if you collect the historical data and tune your percentages accordingly. The expected value provides a good cross-check to the total new program revenue that is currently in your revenue forecast.

The column titled **Close Date** is the salesperson's best estimate of when the customer will award the business to a supplier. A clear metric is needed to convert an opportunity to a design win. As a rule, the first production purchase order should be the design-win trigger as it not only signals the customer has selected you, but that all administrative issues required to generate orders have been resolved.

The column titled **Actions** allows space for a few words to define the next key-action item.

The simple funnel in Figure 2 will need to be customized to your business and expanded accordingly. To complete your funnel definition, start at the left margin and insert columns that support sorting the file to facilitate your review. Columns should be added for any functional group that will be sorting the file, such as product and sales managers and salespeople.

Those readers with a background in medieval philosophy may remember a concept known as "Ockham's razor" from William of Ockham. Ockham's razor states that the best theory is the one with the fewest assumptions.

While William used this tool to rid the world of unneeded metaphysical entities—for example, whether numbers are real, physical things—the concept is invoked here to make the point that simple is always better, particularly when constructing your design-win funnel. It's a fact that the larger the data set maintained, the lower the quality of the data. So, when in doubt, take it out.

Key Point: *When designing your funnel, err on the side of keeping it simple. Increasing the number of data elements, or increasing the complexity of the data definitions, lowers the quality of the data.*

MANAGING THE FUNNEL

Marketing owns the design-win process since they own revenue. As with the revenue forecast, this in no way lessens the accountability of sales to close targeted design wins.

Marketing coordinates strategies and resourcing plans with the sales team and generates a design-win forecast. The sales team is the "execution arm" of marketing to achieve those goals.

As with the processes we've presented in previous chapters, the design-win process requires a process owner to gather updates, publish a consolidated file, and calendar review meetings.

The design-win review meeting should rotate through the marketing team members to allow them to review their product line(s). During the review they should lead their respective discussions and achieve the following:

- **Provide direction to the sales and product support teams.** The product-oriented nature of the meeting provides an excellent opportunity to provide a brief update on product schedules, pricing policy changes, and the priorities that sales should be driving.

- **Ensure strategies and resources are in place to win high potential opportunities.** Of course, most of the meeting should be spent on those few opportunities that will maximize revenue. Also, this meeting is not the place to create individual strategies, but rather to work exceptions, such as open-action items or stages (i.e., milestones) that are past their close dates. Issues that require extended discussion are taken offline.

- **Review the design-win forecast.** Each marketing team member should sort the funnel for their product lines (as shown below) and ensure that the totals reflect what is expected in their revenue forecast.

These three points represent a lot to cover in a short time, so the discussion must be crisp. Like any good review, the meeting should have a moderator who moves the meeting along and takes action items when the team hits a topic that requires a detailed discussion.

Key Point: *As with any review, the meeting should have an owner, such as the relevant sales manager who has the task of keeping the meeting moving forward.*

Design-win reviews are only as good as the follow-through they generate, so it is critical that the process owner publish an updated design-win file with action items following the review.

To prepare for a design-win review meeting, each marketing team member should sort the funnel to show totals for their product lines. Figure 3 sorts the data in Figure 2 to provide a design-win forecast by product line

Customer	Sales	Prod. Line	Product	Volume	ASP		Ext. Value		Total Value		Stage	Close	Actions
A	Person A	Line A	Prod W	1000	$	100	$ 25,000	$	100,000		2	12/10/11	Sampling
B	Person B	Line A	Prod Y	800	$	75	$ 42,000	$	60,000		1	11/25/11	Presentation
					Line A		$ 67,000	$	160,000				
C	Person A	Line B	Prod X	1500	$	150	$ 33,750	$	225,000		3	1/10/12	Passed Eval
D	Person A	Line B	Prod Z	1200	$	50	$ 60,000	$	60,000		4	10/10/11	Closed
					Line B		$ 93,750	$	285,000				
					TOTAL		$ 160,750	$	445,000				

Figure 5.3. Funnel Sorted by Product Line

With this sort, each marketing team member can verify that the opportunities and revenue values committed by the sales team are aligned with the revenue forecast. The view should be sorted by quarters to allow easy comparison with the revenue forecast.

You will learn a lot about the quality of your marketing team by watching how they drive these review meetings. Pay particular attention to the direction they provide to sales at the beginning of their review. Those with good strategies will give clear direction.

Key Point: *The direction provided to the sales team in the design-win review meetings provides an excellent view into the quality of product-line strategies.*

CLOSING DESIGN WINS

Given that sales is responsible for closing design wins, you'll need to ensure that your management program includes an opportunity to review design-win performance.

Account reviews for individual salespeople (discussed in a later chapter) or dedicated design-win reviews with each marketing team represent two different options for you to consider as forums for reviewing the design funnel.

Whichever approach you choose, you, as sales executive, should attend as many reviews as possible. In addition to staying current, you will generate positive tension by challenging open-action items and missed close dates from the last review. In addition to injecting energy into those specific strategies, you'll be reinforcing a culture that makes commitments and keeps them.

An effective review will carefully scrub the following points:

- **Design-Win Forecast**. The design-win forecast committed in the first month of the quarter should be locked in as the forecast for that quarter and reviewed for progress to target.

  This commitment is no less important than the commitment to achieve that quarter's revenue forecast.

- **Total Values**. These values have a tendency to be inflated so make sure to review them against your share position and the customer's market position.

  Also, if your customer's market is dominated by a few major accounts, you should also make sure you don't have more than one customer forecasting to win the same business, as this will generate double counting in the revenue forecast.

- **Close Dates.** These dates are often too aggressive and need to be reviewed carefully, as salespeople have a tendency to use close dates provided by the customer (which are too optimistic). Close dates need to be judged to include a reasonable buffer for schedule slippage.

  Close dates that have slipped multiple times are a red

flag that the program is in trouble. This can be an issue of customer execution or potential problems with your product or the level of support (to be addressed immediately).

- **Strategies.** Confirm that strategies for the most valuable opportunities are sound and on track in terms of schedule. If you have concerns that require detailed discussion, take an action and work it later.

  As the sales executive, the unique value you bring to this discussion is to make sure that scarce applications and engineering resources are allocated to the best opportunities. Many of the action items you take away from a good account review will be around resourcing.

- **Actions.** Of course, your organization's ability to execute is a direct function of its discipline in closing assigned action items, so the status of actions should be a formal part of this or any other review.

Key Point: *Salespeople are optimistic and sometimes naïve, which finds its way into your forecasts in the form of overstated values and overly aggressive close dates for wins and actions. Take the opportunity to lead in the reviews you attend by questioning values and setting the expectation that forecast data must be reasonably justified.*

A review of a salesperson's funnel also provides an opportunity to ensure that they are allocating their time in a way that maintains a steady flow of new design wins. You'll recall from Figure 1 that a design-win funnel starts at the top with a large number of prospects winnowed over time to a few that are closed. Recall that the values in the stage column represent where an opportunity is in the funnel (i.e., where it is in the customer's decision process).

Therefore, a well-balanced funnel will have substantially more opportunities in earlier stages than later stages, giving it a V shape, which will translate to a steady stream of design wins and new revenue. On the other hand, a funnel with a U shape will inevitably inject the dreaded "feast or famine" effect into your revenue stream.

If you review a funnel with a U shaped funnel, the salesperson should be tasked to step up their prospecting activities to increase the number of qualified opportunities and rebalance the pipeline of opportunities.

CHOOSING A PLATFORM

Excel worksheets represent the low end in terms of functionality and cost while Salesforce.com, the customer relationship management (CRM) category leader is at the high end. There are many options in between, including free web-based products or more moderately priced CRMs such as Microsoft CRM.

Below is a brief overview and comparison of Excel versus Salesforce.com (representing both ends of the functionality/cost spectrum) along the lines of cost, functionality, and scalability. As expected, Excel wins on cost and loses on the other parameters. That said, Excel has a surprising amount of capability for managing a funnel and, based on your objectives, may be adequate to your situation.

- **Cost.** A rough but reasonable number for a Salesforce.com license is $750–$1000 per year per user. This number excludes in-house development and maintenance costs. Since you likely have Excel in your business already, it is essentially free.

- **Functionality**. In addition to its spreadsheet capabilities, Excel has a rich feature set to support analysis of the funnel data. For example, pivot tables make it easy to build specific views around any data value such as customers or products. Also, filter buttons can be inserted at the top of the columns making it easy to sort any of the data elements in that particular column.

  One must remember that Excel is simply a spreadsheet and as such only provides a static snapshot of the data so your funnel will start to age the minute it is published. In addition, while it does have a rich feature set for manipulating and presenting the data, you need to be something of a power user to leverage its capabilities or have access to an Excel "wizard" who can help build your files.

Salesforce.com, on the other hand, is a database with a very flexible user interface that allows for powerful representation of the data in many different preset formats, even by casual users.

A report generator supports ad-hoc presentation of the data in any configuration. Dashboards can easily be created to provide a "situation at a glance" of all key metrics for any desired view of the funnel. Each salesperson and product line can (and should) have its own dashboard so the business can be reviewed from any angle at any time.

In Salesforce.com, each customer opportunity has an individual screen that provides space for all relevant data elements. This is a screen that any user can access to get additional information beyond what would be included in the funnel. Data elements include detail on action items, a progress status, and a place to attach relevant documents.

Salesforce.com is a cloud-based application available anytime, anywhere. Salespeople should be required to update the data whenever the status changes on important opportunities to ensure that the data remains current. Having an up to date view of the funnel at their fingertips is a real asset for a sales manager.

- **Scalability.** A reasonable rule of thumb is that Excel will start to breakdown as you approach managing about a dozen salespeople. Salesforce.com has entry-level plans for as few as five users for a few dollars per month per user and provides another option for small teams and budgets.

Salesforce.com supports third-party plug-ins and/or custom developments. If you're considering a CRM implementation, the platform can support all selling processes and functions outside of sales. Tracking quotes, goal development, incentive systems, and human resource applications are just a few of the possibilities.

Key Point: *Small teams who only need to manage the design funnel will likely find Excel adequate for their needs. Scaling to larger teams, multiple product lines or adding additional management processes will drive the need for a CRM such as Salesforce.com.*

ADVANCED FUNNEL MANAGEMENT

This chapter closes out with a few ideas to extend the value of your funnel in the areas of action-item management and long-term forecasting.

Few experiences for a sales executive are more frustrating than completing a productive review meeting only to learn later that the business was lost because action items agreed on by the team were not completed.

To improve the communication of action items, you should couple CRM platforms directly with Microsoft Outlook to allow tasks (i.e., action items) to be launched and tracked for all significant sales opportunities.

This allows team members to get actions and associated reminders in their email inbox, which encourages follow up. In addition, reports can be run on open-action items, which should serve as your starting point for each review meeting. Having the process owner launch action items following a review ensures that actions get published.

Key Point: *Leveraging the capabilities of the CRM to launch, track, and report on open-action items requires little resource and will improve discipline and execution.*

Turning to forecasting, given a limited number of design wins drive your forecast in a major account, it is useful to build a historical model of how revenue from design wins actually ramp into the revenue stream.

To build this model, go back in time as far as data is available and lay the revenue from design wins by opportunity into quarterly buckets. A review of this data will validate the assumptions you've used in building your funnel metrics. For example, this data can be used to validate the time frame assigned to the total value column in your current funnel. This history can also be used to tune the percentages used in your expected-value calculation.

Key Point: *Historical models built from historical data are an effective cross-check to the metrics embedded in your design-win funnel.*

SUMMARY

This chapter concludes our discussion of the processes required to be in control of corporate revenue, both for the current and extended quarters, as well as new design wins.

Our focus now moves to the customer. Implementation of an effective channel strategy that matches customer need should be your first priority, and it is to that topic we now turn.

"The forces of a powerful ally can be useful and good to those who have recourse to them . . . but are perilous to those who become dependent on them."

Niccolo Machiavelli

(May 3, 1469–June 21, 1527)

CHANNEL STRATEGIES

The discussion has been internally focused in previous chapters: sorting out roles and responsibilities and putting processes in place to get revenue and new business wins under control. While it's important to get your internal house in order, the real world is out there in the field with your customers. Your channel strategy defines your "go-to market" plan, so it is crucial to get it right.

My first small company experience was with a memory IC manufacturer. Immediately after joining as VP Sales, I learned that several months prior, the CEO had terminated the company's network of distributors in Asia in favor of one Asia-wide (pan-Asian) distribution partner. The decision was a disaster and resulted in a loss of 30 percent of the company's business. It took two years to replace this revenue.

This lesson reinforces the point of the Machiavelli quotation that opened this chapter, that is, that partners, in this case channel partners, can have a direct impact on whether you succeed or fail.

Key Point: *Your choice of channel partners can be a key part of your success or a limit to your growth, depending on how wisely you choose and manage your partners. In short, effective channel strategies are key to your company's success.*

The topic of sales channels is a broad and complicated one. To keep the discussion manageable, this chapter will start with an overview that provides a taste for the available options. Following the overview, the discussion will focus directly on channels relevant to major accounts with a specific focus on whether to build a dedicated "in-house" sales team or to outsource the function. The role of indirect logistical partners such as distributors will be discussed, and the chapter will wrap up by considering how to select channel partners and manage them for results.

CHANNEL PARTNER OVERVIEW

Figure 1 provides a top level view of sales channels covering transactions from a consumer buying a Smartphone (lower-right corner) to a business to business relationship worth tens of millions of dollars per year (upper-left corner).

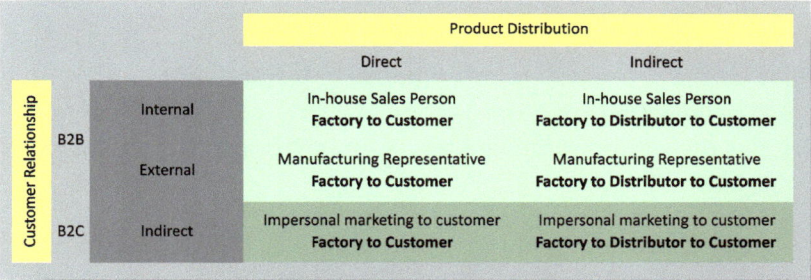

			Product Distribution	
			Direct	Indirect
Customer Relationship	B2B	Internal	In-house Sales Person **Factory to Customer**	In-house Sales Person **Factory to Distributor to Customer**
		External	Manufacturing Representative **Factory to Customer**	Manufacturing Representative **Factory to Distributor to Customer**
	B2C	Indirect	Impersonal marketing to customer **Factory to Customer**	Impersonal marketing to customer **Factory to Distributor to Customer**

Figure 6.1. Top-Level View of Sales Channels Available for Technology Products

The vertical axis, titled **Customer Relationship**, describes the type of entities in the relationship, namely, business to business (B2B) or business to consumer (B2C). The horizontal axis, titled **Product Distribution**, defines how product is delivered to the customer, whether direct from the manufacturer or through an indirect channel partner.

"Direct" means that product ownership only transfers once, from the manufacturer to the customer. Indirect sales refer to transactions where a channel partner, such as a distributor, takes temporary ownership of the product prior to the final sale.

Below is an explanation of each of the boxes in the diagram starting with the B2C relationship in dark green.

BUSINESS TO CONSUMER (B2C)

Buying a computer from Hewlett Packard is a good example of a B2C transaction. The product is purchased either directly from HP online or indirectly from a number of online or retail partners such as Amazon or Best Buy.

A consumer will likely purchase this computer without ever speaking to an HP salesperson. Rather, demand is generated through the "marketing mix," which is a balance of impersonal information sources appropriate for that product including advertising, premium retail space, product reviews, and trade shows.

Another term for going to market in this fashion is "pull marketing," defined as the process of loading indirect channels with inventory prior to product launch, then generating demand with consumers through a marketing campaign which "pulls" the inventory through the channel.

B2C channels are obviously very different from channels to support major accounts, which is our focus. Therefore B2C channels are outside our scope and our discussion of them will end here.

BUSINESS TO BUSINESS (B2B)

With respect to B2B transactions, Figure 1 brackets whether the selling function will be in-sourced or outsourced and whether the customer buys product directly from the manufacturer or from a channel partner who has purchased inventory for resale. Both of these questions are relevant to your choice of channel partners.

The B2B section of Figure 1 is coded in light green and shows all four potential options. The issue of whether the customer buys directly from the manufacturer or indirectly through a channel partner is noted in **bold type**.

Direct Sales

The name gives away the function. The term refers to sales teams that call directly on the customer and therefore own the customer relationship for your company. They are the "one neck to grab" for all issues relating to customer management.

These sales resources can either be on your payroll (in-house) or outsourced to an independent contractor (manufacturer representative).

- **In-House Teams.** The advantage of an in-house sales team is focus and control. As direct employees inside your company, they more easily build trust and better understand how to get things done. On the downside, their salaries are a fixed cost independent of sales volume, so the costs are higher in the early stages of the company when sales are ramping. Because of this upfront cost burden, companies will often enter the market with manufacturer representatives to leverage the benefits of lower cost and improved cash flow, and then transition to an in-house team when volume drives a cost of sales that compares more favorably to outsourcing.
- **Manufacturer Representative Companies (Man Reps).** Man reps sign agreements with a limited number of manufacturers targeted to a particular segment of customers and products. For example, man reps may target companies building wireless systems and therefore choose manufacturers that provide components and subsystems used in the design of those systems. Their portfolio of manufacturers would not include competing products, allowing the man reps to act as the dedicated sales force for all of the companies they represent.

  In this model, purchase orders are placed directly with

the manufacturer and the man reps are paid a commission on sales after the receivables are collected.

The advantages of using man reps are:

- They allow their principals to incur variable rather than fixed costs (they're only paid on what they sell).

- They allow the ability to spread selling costs over all of the manufacturers represented, lowering the average cost to each company.

- They allow improved cash flow since commissions are paid after receivables are collected

These benefits make man reps particularly valuable for cash-strapped start-ups.

When possible, you should choose a man rep that carries complementary lines. This allows the salesperson to "drag" sales of your products along with products from other manufacturers. For example, a power-supply manufacturer would complement any semiconductor supplier making IC's for system-level products since the same engineer will likely use both products in their design.

This strength is also a weakness. Carrying multiple lines also reduces the man rep's focus on your products. Ensuring that your line is resourced properly will always be an issue in this channel.

It doesn't over communicate the point to say that if you're not the #1 or #2 line, your line will not be proactively sold, at best they will "drag" sales of your products with other opportunities for their top lines.

In this case, you will need to generate interest in your major accounts yourself and then use the man rep to manage the local activity.

Key Point: *In a major account environment, a direct selling team, whether internal or outsourced, is a competitive requirement.*

Indirect Sales

Indirect Sales in a B2B context is product sold through companies collectively referred to as "distribution." Distributors are essentially sophisticated logistics companies, managing a large inventory across a large number of products and competing suppliers. Distributors operate under the buy/resale model, meaning the distributor takes title to the product and applies a mark-up on cost for resale to the customer.

In a major account environment, distributors are managed by your direct-selling team, therefore this model is often referred to as "two-tier distribution," meaning the selling team of the distributor and their inventory stands between your sales force and the customer. Depending on the industry, distributors may or may not have salespeople that call on customers in an effort to generate new business.

Given their lack of technical depth and the breadth of the product portfolio they must support, their pre-sales effectiveness is very limited. In a major account, you should consider them as logistics partners only and rely on your direct-selling team to drive your business.

Major accounts often implement a sourcing strategy that procures their steady state or baseline volumes direct from the manufacturer to leverage the lowest cost, and then engage a distributor with local inventory to service any spikes in production. In this model, these distribution partners become part of your sales channel and therefore need to be managed carefully by your direct-sales team to ensure terms (particularly pricing) are consistent across all channel partners.

Key Point: *Distributors are essentially logistics companies that provide local inventory and support to their customers. Major accounts often use* *distributors as logistics partners to support production spikes above their consistent, predictable requirements.*

REGIONAL & MARKET DIFFERENCES

Historically, the US market has featured a well-developed distribution network that hasn't left opportunity for man-rep firms to carry inventory for resale. Therefore most US man reps generate their income solely on revenue booked directly with the manufacturer and then collecting a commission on those sales.

Asia and Europe have evolved differently. Given the language and cultural issues across those geographies, Pan Asian and European distribution companies have been slow to develop, creating an opportunity for smaller companies to provide local inventory. To fill this need, some man reps (known as "stocking reps") will purchase and hold a limited amount of inventory for key customers for products they are confident will sell.

Stocking reps are usually more willing to represent smaller, emerging companies than man reps that are only commission-based because the initial, modest volumes generated by smaller companies represent a good source of revenue and cash flow when supported through a buy/resale model.

Some markets have evolved in a way where man reps provide additional service such as pre and post applications support, product maintenance or other services.

Key Point: *Channels have evolved differently across geographic regions. These differences need to be taken into account when building your strategy.*

EXAMPLE CHANNEL PLAN

The previous section provided an overview of the available options for direct and indirect coverage of your customers. The example provided below will describe the decision process for building out your direct-selling team, which is the most important decision you will make when building a major accounts program.

To get started, clear marketing objectives are required to build an effective channel plan. You'll need to work with your marketing team to align on a plan that provides:

- **Served Available Market (SAM).** By definition, SAM represents the revenue achieved if you have 100 percent share of a market assuming no constraints on your ability to deliver.

  A SAM analysis that breaks out major customers in addition to competitors highlights immediate targets to build revenue. Your share of the SAM represents your market share, so this analysis needs to be regularly updated to track your progress in the account.

- **Revenue Goals**. The SAM analysis, along with a view of how competitive the product portfolio is against competition, ability to scale volume, and other considerations are judged to build reasonable revenue goals.

  Revenue goals should be broken out by geography, major customer, and key product lines so all stakeholders have clear targets.

- **Complete Products.** A complete product includes the product itself (what the customer buys) and everything required to make and support the sale.

  This includes a clear-value proposition, effective pricing, and required application support (data sheets, technical support, etc.). Understanding what is already resourced in the marketing plan makes clear what additional resourcing will be required to implement your channel plan.

Key Point: *The first step in building a channel plan is developing clear marketing objectives.*

The marketing plan and SAM analysis will identify geographic "centers of gravity" where salespeople should be located. Obviously, salespeople should be physically located as close to their customers as possible.

When deciding whether to build an in-house team or use man reps, the first consideration is cost of sales (see example in Figure 2). The example assumes the in-house major accounts salesperson bears a fully loaded cost of $150K USD. For the man reps, a 10 percent commission is assumed, paid in the same quarter as revenue is recognized.

(K$'s)		Q1		Q2		Q3		Q4		Q5		Q6		Q7		Q8
Revenue	$	-	$	-	$	200	$	300	$	500	$	800	$	1,200	$	1,700
Man Rep@ 10%	$	-	$	-	$	20	$	30	$	50	$	80	$	120	$	170
Man Rep Cum	$	-	$	-	$	20	$	50	$	100	$	180	$	300	$	470
In-House Cost	$	36	$	36	$	36	$	36	$	36	$	36	$	36	$	36
In-House Cum	$	36	$	72	$	108	$	144	$	180	$	216	$	252	$	288
Delta	$	(36)	$	(72)	$	(88)	$	(94)	$	(80)	$	(36)	$	48	$	182

Figure 6.2. Cash-Flow Analysis of a Man Rep versus a Single In-House Salesperson

With these assumptions, Figure 2 indicates that it takes almost two years into the product rollout before an in-house sales team makes sense purely from a cost-of-sales perspective.

Therefore, if you're in a small company, cost of sales and cash flow may make man reps the only option to launch your program. Another advantage for small companies is that with teams already in place, man reps can provide immediate coverage of your customers.

Note that Figure 2 doesn't assume improved revenues from a dedicated, more-focused in-house team. This can be an important factor in your decision given that some major accounts strongly prefer to be supported by in-house teams. If your revenue plan is focused on a very few customers, and better yet, if they're in the same geography, the additional upfront costs of an in-house team may generate a good return.

Decisions around product or application support, customer service, and/or the inside sales functions are outside the scope of this chapter.

Key Point: *A well-designed channel plan makes effective trade-offs between the initial cost benefits available from man reps and the focus gained from dedicated in-house sales teams.*

The SAM analysis, revenue plan detail, additional resourcing required should be combined with any other goals such as high-potential design wins into a channel plan document that can be used both for communication and follow-up purposes.

HIRING MANUFACTURER REPS

You are only as strong as the team that you run with. To that point, hiring man reps is similar to hiring salespeople, that is, interviews and references are the primary sources of information to guide your decision.

Just as when hiring salespeople, a clear requirements document is needed to ensure that you and those involved in the interview process are clear about your expectations. These expectations should include coverage requirements, resources, and skill levels that the winning man rep should provide.

Below are points to consider when selecting man reps:

Independent references. References provided by the candidate can be helpful, but nowhere near as helpful as an independent source. To that end, references not provided by the candidate are your best source of information.

Interview as a *team*. Interviewing is best conducted as a team sport. Involving stakeholders in the decision brings different perspectives to the interview, improves the selection process, and generates automatic buy-in for the new hire. This is particularly important in sales, where the man reps will effectively work across functions in the company. To that end, your marketing team should be part of the interview team.

If you use a team interviewing process, a simple matrix is an effective way to organize the output. The example provided in Figure 3 takes an average score across the interviewers (top section) weighted for the hiring characteristics drawn from the job description.

Scoring 1-10	Technical	Communication	Contacts	Can Close	Total
Candidate 1	3	8	2	8	21
Candidate 2	9	4	8	3	24
Candidate 3	2	9	2	8	21
Candidate 4	8	3	9	2	22
Weight	0.2	0.4	0.1	0.3	1
Candidate 1	0.6	3.2	0.2	2.4	6.4
Candidate 2	1.8	1.6	0.8	0.9	5.1
Candidate 3	0.4	3.6	0.2	2.4	6.6
Candidate 4	1.6	1.2	0.9	0.6	4.3

Figure 6.3. Sample Interview Matrix Showing Weighted Summaries for Each Candidate

Of course you won't make your hiring decision off of a spreadsheet, but this analysis does help clarify your thinking and provides a tool to facilitate communication between those that participated in the interviews.

Key Point: *Hiring decisions are critical and by definition based on relatively little information. This underlines the importance of involving as many sources of evaluation as possible.*

Require a business plan. When interviewing man reps, the meeting should begin with their presentation of a business plan for your line. They should provide a revenue profile and a strategy to drive the results that they believe they can generate for your company.

The best plans will provide a SAM analysis, potential revenue for targeted customers, and a resource plan. You'll learn a lot about their ability to build a strategy along with getting commitments on revenues and resourcing that you can hold them accountable to later.

Key Point: *Requiring a potential channel partner to present a business plan as part of the screening process allows you to gauge how well they understand their business and sets expectations for results if they're hired.*

The most important criteria in evaluating a man rep are the quality of their salespeople and the processes used to run the business (these usually go together). You can get some sense for skill sets by interviewing team members, but the real test is how they are positioned in their accounts and what kind of market share they are driving for the current suppliers they represent.

Willingness to resource your line properly is important and can be a particular concern if one manufacturer dominates the candidate company's revenues. On the flip side, a man rep that has just lost a manufacturer can be an excellent fit. Bottom line, you need to be comfortable that the man rep you select is hungry enough to actively resource and drive your product line when you're not watching.

As mentioned earlier, the companies that the man rep represents should not have competing products. Ideally, the products are complementary, that is, that customers would evaluate a product from one manufacturer at the same time they are evaluating a product from another. Good salespeople love these synergies as they can sell multiple products on the same sales call and can offer bundled pricing when quoting business. Further, a lead for one product is usually a lead for complementary products as well.

MANAGING MANUFACTURERS REPS

As with any other relationship, getting started on the right foot is important. Specifically, you need to get acceptable terms in the contract and set the right expectations regarding results. Regarding your agreements, they should be one-sided in favor of you, the manufacturer. Except in start-ups where you lack leverage, you can and should adopt a "take it or leave it" approach to terms.

These agreements should be kept simple and held to a few pages. There are only a few specific terms that you need to make sure you get right:

- Commission Rate. An appropriate rate is one that compares favorably to your cost of an in-house resource performing the same service. With this in mind, small and/or new companies usually pay 15 percent and higher on revenue since the man reps may be making a significant investment up front.

  On the other end of the spectrum, high-volume relationships can go as low as 1 percent to provide a competitive rate against an in-house team. Remember, man reps will value the opportunity based on potential commissions versus cost, so the commission percentage only matters relative to that.

  Negotiating different commission rates for different customers or products is appropriate. For example, if the man rep is supporting a customer with substantial existing revenue, this volume should be at a relatively low rate (which may still generate substantial commission dollars) while new customers would be at a higher rate. You may also want to provide higher rates as an incentive for products that are more difficult to sell or for new products where the initial revenue wins are crucial.

- Termination. However it is worded, make sure that you have the ability to terminate the relationship for any reason (known as termination for convenience). Your channel strategy is too important to be held hostage to a third party. You need to be able to make a change whenever and for whatever reason you feel appropriate. It is standard to provide a notice of termination typically in the 30- to 60-day range.

- Termination Privileges. Like an employee, man reps should have some benefits upon termination to allow them to shift resources to other opportunities and get some benefit for business they've generated. It is common to allow them to ship backlog with ship dates within 90 days of the termination date.

  Termination privileges are the most hotly negotiated terms after the commission rate. If you're a small company you may need to flex a bit here. Granting a grace period longer than six months should require extraordinary circumstances. Enduring a grace period longer than six months forces you to either endure an extended transition period with an unmotivated partner or to pay double commissions.

- Payment Terms. Man reps should be paid after your company gets paid. This ensures that they are motivated to see that receivables are collected.

- Changes to Terms. The contract should allow you to change any of the commercial terms at any time. For example, you may want to bring on a new man rep and reduce the size of his or her territory, or, you may even be required to change commission rates due to your prospects. This flexibility is not often required, but when it is, you'll be glad you made provision for it.

Key Point: *Agreements with man reps should provide flexibility to make changes in terms at any time. These kinds of terms are standard in the industry and should be in your agreements.*

MAN REP REVIEWS

The management dictum "you only get what you measure" is certainly true when it comes to man reps. Frequency of reviews is a function of the size of the relationship. If a man rep is managing a large or strategic customer, reviews should be held monthly. At a minimum, reviews should be held quarterly to make sure the teams stay aligned and updated on status. Agenda items should include the following:

- Status of actions from the previous meeting.
- Revenue and new business review: a discussion of progress to revenue and design win targets allows you to gauge performance and surface issues that need to be addressed in product or technical support.
- Resourcing: like any small company, man reps are strapped for resources so ensuring they're resourcing your line properly is always a discussion point and a constant battle. Stick with it, the squeaky wheel does indeed get the grease.
- Actions. You should manage man reps assuming they will forget about you when you leave. Make sure to take careful notes on actions and issues and promptly publish them after the review.

Manage man reps as you would manage employees; be tough on results, but be fair and minimize surprises.

Key Point: *The management dictum "you only get what you measure" is also true when managing channel partners, so make sure you put a review process in place and stick to it.*

SUMMARY

When it comes to channel partners there are many business models available to you as the sales executive. In a major account environment, the major decision is between outsourcing the function to manufacturer representatives or whether to build an in-house team.

Small companies usually start with man reps because the early costs are lower, and then transition to in-house teams as the business builds. Distribution partners are also available to provide local inventory and support if needed.

When engaging man reps, you'll need to make sure you get very flexible and favorable terms in your agreements. You'll be glad you did later.

In addition to processes that manage the overall business, account reviews and strategic account plans set expectations and plans for individual sales territories and major accounts. We'll turn to that topic next.

"Planning is bringing the future into the present so that you can do something about it now."

Alan Lakein

ACCOUNT PLANNING

Previous chapters have presented processes designed to track and drive the business from the top down and align stakeholders on actions.

Account planning, on the other hand, provides an opportunity for salespeople and their managers to develop a plan and drive it up the management chain for alignment and resourcing.

In traditional manufacturing businesses, technology moved relatively slowly and the most important information—regarding markets and the company's plan—was held by management. It was management's task to drive those ideas down to the front line of the company for execution. A very top down model.

In a technology company, however, the most important information was held by individual technical staff, who lived on the leading edge and who were positioned well down the organization chart from executive management. In this case, information in technology companies is required to *flow up* to management, and quickly, given the rate of change, so that they can make informed decisions. To encourage this upward flow of information Andy Grove CEO of Intel during their salad days, eliminated executive washrooms and parking spaces.

The same is true in sales. The sales team is closest to the customer's needs and the movement of competition. An effective account planning process can provide the needed upward flow of information regarding changes with customers and markets to management.

Key Point: *Account plans provide an opportunity for sales staff to keep management abreast of changes with customers and competitors and drive for resources and needed change. Information gathered in the account review process can benefit all functions in the company.*

These benefits are in addition to the primary objective of account planning, which is to ensure that all critical accounts have a well-considered and well-resourced plan to drive growth and improve customer satisfaction.

For our purposes, this chapter will break account planning into two distinct processes, each with different objectives:

- **Account Reviews**: The scope of an account review is an individual salesperson's total set of customers. Account reviews are brief, regular updates that take a short-term (roughly 90-day) view.
- **Strategic Account Plans:** These plans do a deep dive on one major account. The plan takes a long-term view and aligns with the corporate planning horizon (usually 36 months or longer).

  While the sales team drives the strategic account planning process (working very closely with marketing), the plans should reflect objectives across all functions and therefore be the company's plan, not just the view from the sales function.

Key Point: *Account planning should be broken into two processes, one with a short-term view (account reviews) and the other with a long-term view (strategic account plans). The difference in planning horizons drives the need for different processes.*

ACCOUNT REVIEWS

Account reviews focus on performance to the current and next-quarter targets committed in the revenue and design-win forecasts. The reviews are held regularly, usually monthly, so keeping preparation to a minimum is important.

A manager should view the account review as his or her monthly opportunity to put direct focus on a particular salesperson and his or her objectives. This tool becomes increasingly important as a sales manager's span of control increases.

An account review should provide:

- **A platform for upward communication.** The account review is the only forum for a salesperson to present a summary view of his or her accounts. It provides an opportunity to post progress to targets, request corporate resources, influence timely decisions, and highlight important issues.
- **Progress to current and next-quarter targets.** By definition these are the salesperson's assigned budget or quota.
- **Status of strategies for closing new business.** These should focus on high potential opportunities.
- **Next actions/resources needed.** The review begins with the status of actions from the last review and ends by summarizing actions for follow-up.

The template for this meeting should take the salesperson no more than an hour to prepare. This can be achieved if the template is designed primarily to reuse available reports.

For example, revenue and design-win data should be direct imports from the revenue and design-win reports. In a company with corporate software, like an ERP System or Salesforce, the template should consist of reports available directly from those programs.

Key Point: *Account reviews should be high impact in terms of the information communicated but low impact in terms of the preparation required.*

By keeping preparation to a minimum, these reviews can and should be held monthly and should be no longer than 45 minutes each. Keeping a brisk pace will discourage getting into the details but still provide adequate time to get a good view of the business.

Since reviews are held monthly, they should become a regular part of the calendar and should be scheduled for the same time each month. The salesperson's manager and any other team members relevant to agenda items should attend.

As the sales executive, you should attend as many of these reviews as possible. Not only are these reviews your best opportunity to understand what is going on with customers, but it's likely that you and any other management attending will pick up on action items related to resourcing or problems needing immediate resolution. In addition, your attendance also signals to the salesperson that his or her customers are a priority.

Key Point: *Account reviews are the most leveraged use of a sales executive's time. Well-prepared account reviews are a gold mine of information about progress with customers, barriers to winning important new business and the quality of effort within the sales team.*

ACCOUNT REVIEW MEETING

A good account review can be prepared in about half-a-dozen slides. The review package should include:

Highlights/Lowlights and Last Review's Actions
Consider the highlights/lowlights as headlines, which allow the salesperson to present the major messages for that review. This is also a good place to insert the status of action items from the previous review.

Revenue Forecast-These slides need to be tailored to the specific salesperson, depending on how many customers and product lines are reviewed. Your sales-reporting system should provide a "canned" or standard report that can be accessed any time a salesperson wants to check progress to quota and can be used directly for the account review.

Design-Win Opportunities-This slide should also be a simple cut-and-paste from a standard report as well. At a minimum, each opportunity (row) should show the total and expected values, close date, and stage position (see the chapter titled "Closing New Business" for an example template). This slide should also indicate progress to that quarter's design-win forecast and relevant headlines.

Service Metrics-This section should be provided by operations or customer service (also should be a canned report) and include key-service metrics needed to measure customer satisfaction. On-time shipping performance and product return statistics are relevant examples.

Issues-The salesperson is allowed one slide to articulate resources needed and majors problems to be solved. This slide represents what writers call "the wisdom," or where the key takeaways are located.

Examples will include product or service problems that are restricting growth as well as barriers to sales productivity, like non-value added requests for information from marketing. Management should take action items away from this discussion.

This is the salesperson's meeting so he or she should set the agenda and run the meeting.

That said, these reviews need to be short for the sake of efficiency. With good preparation and by always moving briskly through the topics (taking actions for more discussion later when needed), these reviews can comfortably be done in 40 minutes; maybe a few minutes less. The last slide is the exception. Proper pacing will leave a third of the time to allow discussion of critical points.

 Key Point: *Avoid the common mistake of agonizing over details in the numbers and leaving inadequate time to engage profitable discussion on the last slide, which is where the salesperson has the opportunity to present his or her best opportunities and most pressing problems.*

Lastly, like any of the processes presented in these newsletters, review meetings are only as good as the resulting follow-up. Therefore, reviews should begin by discussing the status of actions from the last review and end with a summary of actions.

STRATEGIC ACCOUNT PLANS

While the purpose behind an account review is to provide brief and regular updates on performance to targets, a strategic account plan is just that—a plan—and one with a focus on the time horizon of the corporate planning process. The longer time horizon drives a focus on important, but not urgent, issues that often get too little of our time. With the constant crush to meet the quarter, we need to force dialogue around such key issues as planning to enter new product segments or building better executive relationships with customers.

These plans are a lot of work for everyone involved and particularly for your sales and marketing team. You'll also need a reasonable commitment from your executives to attend reviews and take action items, so be sure to get agreement from everyone who will be involved. Given the amount of effort involved, the return is only there for those very few accounts that really drive your business and that you genuinely consider strategic.

The senior operational staff of the company should attend these reviews, given the quality of these customers and the strategic topics covered. Senior staff not only needs to hear this information, they are the only ones that can drive the kind of initiatives presented. Said another way, the requests made in these reviews require resources (such as new logistical programs or new products), and the senior staff controls them.

About the only way to get the right audience for these reviews is to schedule them on the back end of corporate operations reviews when the senior staff is already together. If these reviews are held monthly, the practice of scheduling them with operations reviews would allow all of your critical customers to be reviewed. You may only need to schedule a review every other month.

Key Point: *Strategic account plans are a lot of work, so make sure to get agreement from all participants. Given the effort, this process should* *only focus on those few customers that drive the business and that are considered strategic by the management team.*

STRATEGIC PLANNING OBJECTIVES

Set "Stretch" Revenue Goals-Take the opportunity to stretch your team's thinking by setting a revenue goal that is considerably larger than current expectations. A stretch target drives the team to get creative when proposing opportunities and programs that could achieve the target.

Drive Executive Relationships-These relationships are one of the important but not urgent objectives this process must drive. You never really appreciate the importance of good executive relationships until they are needed and by then it is too late to develop them.

Source for New Product/Program Proposals-Well-chosen "stretch" revenue targets will drive requests for new products or service programs. These new initiatives, as approved by the executive team, should be fed directly into the corporate planning process.

This process helps your team's ability to think, write, and work cross functionally like nothing else. As a result, strategic account plans are a great way to build the sales and marketing team's business skills. You'll likely be surprised at who does well and who struggles with this process.

The ability to plan is a critical management skill. The insight developed while evaluating your team's participation will be helpful when evaluating staff for promotion. The company's sense of team will also be enhanced as a result of the cross-functional work required to build each plan.

Key Point: *Building strategic account plans will build your team's professional skills by stressing their ability to think clearly, write, and work cross functionally.*

Overview Section

The overview section will provide a baseline of information that is particularly useful for attendees who know relatively little about the customer and will provide context for the rest of the plan. The overview section should include:

- **Key Figures** (1-2 slides). Include the customer's total corporate revenues and detail for relevant divisions. Include other facts relevant to those reading the plan such as the number of employees, locations, etc.

- **Customer Organization Chart** (1 slide). Try to keep this to one slide.

- **Revenue Summary** (1 slide). Break out revenues with the customer by-product line. The best time frame to represent will depend on your business, but a good rule of thumb for a company that develops products is to show the two previous years and four rolling quarters of forecast.

- **Served Available Market.** The concept "served available market" (SAM) was first presented in the chapter titled "Channels." Recall that SAM represents the business available to you for a product or product category. Specifically, the SAM is revenue assuming you have 100 percent of the business for that product or category. SAM is presented as a matrix, with competitors listed across the top and your relevant products down the side with the numbers summing to total SAM in the lower right-hand corner.

  An accurate SAM chart, better than any other analysis, provides a snapshot of where you stand relative to your competitors and therefore highlights areas where an effective strategy could provide short-term growth.

- **Trends** (1 slide). List trends that are impacting the customer's business. These could be competitive, regulatory, or technology-oriented trends. The purpose for listing these trends is to provide context for the objectives in the plan. Specifically, objectives should tie to these trends, i.e., they should reduce risk or leverage an opportunity.

Key Point: *An overview providing an introductory view of the customer is required to provide context and to provide a baseline of information given the broad audience that will see the plan.*

Objectives, Strategies, and Tactics

This section will start by defining the terms *objective, strategy* and *tactic,* as these terms are used quite differently across the literature. For our purposes these terms are defined as follows:

- **Objective**: A statement of purpose, a target, or goal. Objectives must be measurable. By contrast, a strategy describes how the objective will be obtained. When choosing objectives, think clearly whether a potential objective is really a strategy, as the distinction can be somewhat subjective.

  A good guideline is that an objective is broad enough to require a number of initiatives or strategies to be implemented. For example, getting a design win for a new product with a new customer may be a good objective, as you'll need to execute strategies to build relationships, strategies to position products, etc., to position your company for the win.

  The trends identified in the overview are a potential source of objectives. You should also visualize how you want to be positioned in the account at the end of the planning horizon relative to the trends presented in the overview as a cross-check to the alignment of the proposed objectives.

- **Strategies:** Strategies are those specific initiatives that achieve the objective. For example, under an objective to improve operational execution, strategies might include implementing an inventory-management program or developing a program with the customer to better manage product returns. Like objectives, strategies must be measurable.

- **Tactics**: These are the collection of specific actions or tasks required to implement a specific strategy. A tactic states the specific deliverable, who will do it, and when it will be accomplished.

Key Point: *To cross-check that the right objectives are in the plan, visualize where you want to be with the customer at the end of the planning horizon versus the trends presented in the introduction.*

A simple analogy to summarize the relationship between objectives, strategies, and tactics is to think of scaling a wall. Choosing the objective is the act of choosing which wall to scale. Strategies are choosing the right tools, e.g., ladders versus ropes, the path of ascent, etc. Finally, tactics are the physical activities required to climb the wall.

Good objectives are win/win for you and the customer. To ensure win/win objectives, make sure to write them from the customer's perspective by asking the question "What kind of supplier does this customer want us to be?"

Figure 1 presents a sample plan objective (from the customer's view) with supporting strategies.

Operational Improvement

- Objective:
  Improve operational metric on customer's scorecard from yellow to green by __.
  Customer's costs to source product and repair product will decrease. Improved
  operational support will increase our share of business.

- Strategy #1
  Improve performance to customer requested ship dates to 90% monthly through
  implementation of a value added inventory program.

- Strategy #2
  Develop jointly resourced program with customer to reduce Product Returns to
  less than 1%.

- Strategy #3
  Improve responsiveness by launching a customer portal providing access to order
  status and tracking information

Figure 7.1. Sample Plan Slide with an Objective and Supporting Strategies

Tactics should be presented in a slide behind the strategies. Tactics by definition are measureable, with an owner and date for completion identified.

STRATEGIC REVENUE PLAN

The sales and marketing teams work together closely to build the revenue plan. The revenue plan requires consolidation of three views:

1. **Current Production**-Start with the current approved forecast and extend it to the end of the plan-time horizon building in the assumption that the revenue stream will increasingly decline in time. This forecast will include the baseline revenue from products currently qualified and in production and include new business in the design-win funnel, which is

forecasted to close and ramp into production.

Of course, this current production revenue will decline over time and this will need to be factored into the later quarters.

For example, if the quarters beyond your four-quarter forecast have historically needed to replace about a third of the business each year to keep revenues flat, a reasonable assumption would be to reduce those out quarters by an average of about 8 percent per quarter to the end of the plan period. This current production forecast provides the foundation upon which the next two views are added.

2. **New Business from the Existing Product Portfolio**-The second view includes new business wins from products currently in production but not included in the current production forecast. New products must be resourced and have launch dates published internally. The design-win funnel is the source for these numbers.

   Obviously, these numbers will carry higher risk than the current forecast numbers given they are farther out in time.

3. **Strategic Products**-The third and final view includes revenue from products not currently on the product roadmap. `This view includes products with a reasonable technology fit but which are not currently resourced.

   Marketing should own this section of the revenue plan, given the charter for the product roadmap lies here. The product ideas and numbers should align with the marketing plan and in that sense strategic account plans provide an excellent cross-check.

   This view has the potential to generate very productive discussion when these plans are presented to management. Any conclusions reached can then be folded into the company's product-development process.

Key Point: *The strategic products portion of the revenue plan will generate meaningful discussion during review of the plan, as it will propose new, high leverage products not currently in the product roadmap.*

These three views are added together to provide the strategic forecast. Figure 2, below, shows an example summary view.

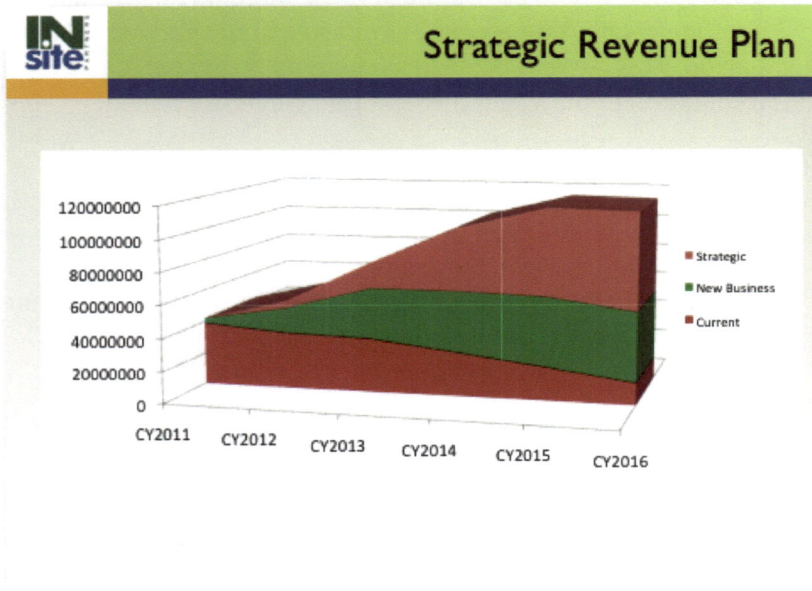

Figure 7.2. Example Strategic Revenue Plan Summarizing the Three Views of Revenue

Figure 2 provides only the shape of the revenue plan. The plan assumptions and, more importantly, the call to action to resource these new initiatives should be provided in a few slides behind this graphic.

Given the importance of strategic account plans, you as the sales executive need to manage the overall process. These plans are a lot of work and your direct involvement will underline the importance of the process to all of those who will put in the many hours required to build them. Also, good plans will certainly tax the business planning skills of even your best staff so you need to be available to "unstick" them when they run into difficulty.

Executive Alignment/Process Kickoff-The objectives of the planning process should be presented to the executive team to understand their issues and gather their support. Dates should be selected for the final plan reviews so that these can be presented at the team kick-off meeting.

With the executive team aligned, teams are chosen, trained, and the process launched. The account manager is designated as the team leader and is responsible for managing the development of each plan. In addition to the marketing team, who will be directly involved, team members should be added from other functions as needed. For example, if you're confident that there is opportunity to improve the position in the account by improved execution, operations should be added to the team.

You should present expectations for content and timelines at a kick-off meeting. Make sure everyone comes away with a clear understanding of the difference between objectives and strategies and what must be included in the strategic portion of the revenue plan. Don't miss the opportunity to generate some "positive tension" in the team by providing the final presentation review dates.

Key Point: *This process will generate tension. Immature managers will try to smooth that away, good managers won't avoid it, and great managers will figure out how to channel the heat from the friction into energy that pushes the company forward.*

Plan Development-The objectives, strategies, tactics (OSTs), and strategic revenue plan should be developed in parallel. As mentioned above, the account manager should manage the overall project and take ownership of the overview section and the OSTs. In parallel, sales and marketing team members should jointly develop the revenue plan, with marketing owning the strategic revenue view.

You must have regular reviews along the way to identify teams that are struggling. As a quality check, hold a formal dry run of the presentation prior to the executive review. In addition to making final improvements to the plan, it will build the team's confidence for their presentation to the executive team.

Key Point: *Regular reviews of the draft plans and enough dry runs to resolve issues are critical to ensuring that the quality of the final plans is consistent.*

EXECUTIVE REVIEW AND ALIGNMENT

Strategic account planning should be a formal part of the corporate planning process. Presentation of the plans should be scheduled so that new initiatives and product ideas are folded into the corporate planning process.

The presentation of each plan will require a full hour to allow adequate time for questions. The most fruitful discussion will happen around the OSTs and potential new product ideas. As always, action items must be published following the review.

After the plan presentation and with the team aligned, the plan should be presented to the customer's executive management. Customers appreciate the opportunity to have input into their supplier's planning process. This provides a great way to get validation and customer buy in.

The plans should be redone each year as part of the corporate planning cycle with a refresh at the six-month mark.

SUMMARY

Account planning is an essential part of your sales management process-portfolio as it provides a way to monitor progress of each salesperson's overall customer set and allows for communication between the sales team and management.

Two separate processes are needed to cover both the short- and long-term view of the business. Account reviews are held monthly, with a focus on execution to targets for the following 90 days.

Strategic account plans align with the corporate planning horizon, usually in the 24- to 36-month range. Account plans include important but often overlooked objectives, such as building executive engagements and entering new product categories.

Strategic account plans involve all customer-facing functions and as a result create a corporate plan for that customer. Given that these plans require a substantial effort, they should only be prepared for those few customers that are truly considered strategic.

With all of our key sales processes in place we will now turn to the discussion of incentive systems; an important but historically frustrating topic for most sales executives.

"Call it what you will, incentives are what get people to work harder."

Nikita Khrushchev

(April 15, 1894–September 11, 1971)

INCENTIVE PLANS

If, of all people, one of our most famous Communists, signed on to the power of incentives, then there must be something to it. The trick is in developing cost-effective incentives that actually work. Too frequently, truth in advertising would require incentive plans to be labeled as "dis-incentive plans."

A few years ago I was in that very position. Our commission plan was a simple one; at the beginning of each fiscal half targets were set for the coming two quarters and then paid on performance to those targets with an accelerated payout to any team member who exceeded his or her numbers. The problem was that the fortunes of each major customer often changed quickly, making it difficult to forecast short-term results.

As a result, a large payout on the upside or miss to the downside was too often a result of some large, unforecasted change in a customer's business. The sales team members weren't motivated because if they beat the plan significantly they felt it was deserved (that's human nature for you), but if a customer's business tanked they felt they were being unfairly punished. In sum, rewards were not clearly tied to results from either the perspective of management or the sales team.

Not happy with our plan, we sent our HR partner to do some research and get training on compensation plans. Her most shocking finding from the surveys was that while most companies had plans similar to ours, less than a quarter of them were happy with the results.

Why would so many companies stick with plans they weren't happy with? In our case we stuck with our plan because it was simple to devise and explain and straightforward to budget, not because it motivated the sales team to grow the business. This was likely the case for other companies.

We took this to heart and set about redesigning our plan. It required a significant investment of our time, but in the end we learned that you can build effective incentive plans if you take time to do it right.

This process must start by finding objectives that are clear and then having the patience to sift through many options until you find one that models your business environment and drives your team toward your objectives.

Key Point: *Sales incentive plans can have a positive impact on your business if the plan is consistent with corporate objectives and your culture; otherwise, you likely have a "dis-incentive" plan. There isn't a middle ground.*

This chapter will focus on incentive plans in the context of a major-accounts selling program. Actual plan design is outside the scope of this chapter. The goal here is to provide a way for thinking through which elements to include and how to administer the plan as it rolls out.

A few definitions:

- **Total Compensation**—Base salary plus incentive payouts at 100 percent of plan.
- **Plan Target**—Performance required to earn 100 percent payout to the plan. A target is established for each plan element, such as revenue, new business wins (i.e., design wins, etc.).
- **Plan Element**—Specific plan component. In addition to revenue, your plan may have elements (potential payouts) for other components, such as design wins, gross margin, etc.
- **Bonus**—A payout related to a one-time achievement, which is in addition to incentive payouts included in total compensation.

Development of an effective plan starts with the executive team getting aligned on priorities. These priorities should be taken from (or at least consistent with) your corporate plan. Specifically, a point of view needs to be developed regarding:

- **Financial Priorities**—Understanding the relative priority of revenue, gross margin, and new-business wins will guide decisions regarding those elements that should be included in the plan and how they should be weighted.
- **Strategic Products**—The decision needs to be made whether any specific products should be considered more important than others in terms of design wins and should therefore receive priority in the plan.
- **Executive Involvement**—Some CEOs participate in the plan through programs such as a President's Club. These programs can be an effective way of reinforcing the importance of hitting revenue targets, provided the executive personally drives them.

After aligning with the executive team on priorities, the list of guiding principles should be crosschecked against the plan as it is developed. A sample list of guiding principles is presented in Figure 1 below.

Incentive Priorities	#1—Revenue growth
	#2—Closing new business.
	#3—Gross-margin percentage
Executive Focus	The plan emphasizes that these priorities are critical and will receive regular CEO review and participation.

Figure 8.1. Sample Set of Guiding Principles for Development of an Incentive Plan

Compensation is a topic where CEOs have very definite views. These views will vary widely and sometimes violently from CEO to CEO, so if you don't involve them early in the process, odds are good you'll be sent back to the drawing board when you present for approval.

Some CEOs feel that the sales team should be incentivized only on revenue, with the team therefore biased to book every potential piece of business, while at the other end of the spectrum some feel that pricing decisions should be made primarily on gross-margin contribution. In other words, if it doesn't hit a margin target it shouldn't be brought in for consideration.

These two views on revenue and margin, and all those in between, will generate very different sets of guiding principles. There may be other considerations, such as whether sales should be responsible for expediting payment of receivables. This again highlights the need to get the executive team, and particularly the CEO, aligned before starting to choose the plan elements.

Key Point: *Prior to developing the plan, taking the time to align priorities with the executive team will allow you to build a list of guiding principles that can be used to validate the plan as it is developed.*

PLAN COMPONENTS

Base vs. Incentive Split

A number of issues should be considered when deciding what percentage of a salesperson's compensation should be put "at risk." The most important consideration is the amount of direct control the salesperson has over the sale.

Take the example of selling door-to-door. The salesperson either closes the deal on the spot or very likely doesn't get the sale. Given that the salesperson has substantial impact at the point of sale, all or at least most of his or her compensation should be in incentive payment, that is, "at risk." The harder they work, the better they get at closing business and consequently, the more they make.

Selling to a major account is very different, as it involves a broad list of activities, some of which are related to supporting the existing revenues rather than generating new business. In addition, the sales team should make decisions in ways that foster a long-term relationship, as opposed to the door-to-door salesperson who will likely never see the customer again.

This breadth of responsibility raises these kinds of issues:

- **Revenue Carryover**—The longer the life cycle of your business (product life cycle or contract life), the more effort is spent managing existing run rate. A longer life cycle argues for a higher percentage to the base.
- **Selling Cycle**—Shorter selling cycles suggest that more compensation should be at risk, as payment is closer to the start of the selling process where it can influence behavior.
- **Management Control**—The larger the percentage of compensation "at risk," the less control management will have over the day-to-day activities of the salesperson since the salesperson will have more incentive to maximize their short-term payouts.
- **Cost of Sales Management**—Incentive payouts introduce variability into cost of sales. If operating to a fixed budget is important, variability is reduced with a higher percentage allocated to base salary.

Considering these factors, major account plans, which usually have longer selling cycles and need to foster longer-term decision making, are usually weighted more toward base than incentive, with base salary accounting for 60 percent to 80 percent of total compensation.

After deciding on the base vs. incentive split, plan development can turn toward the components themselves.

Key Point: *The decision regarding how total compensation should be split between base salary and incentive compensation should consider a number of factors, including the amount of control the salesperson exerts over the decision at the point of sale.*

Revenues, Bookings, and Gross Margins

Driving revenue is the primary objective for any sales team, so performance-to-revenue targets will represent an important component of every plan. To ensure alignment between sales and other functions in the company, the total revenue target for the sales team (the VP sales target) should be the same target the company has committed to stakeholders, and that is used for any other corporate incentive programs.

Several issues need to be considered when deciding whether or how to include gross-margin performance. The bias of your executives, as well as the maturity of your team—specifically their ability to think bottom line—needs to be considered. Again, it is a question of direction. Putting the focus primarily on top-line expansion leans toward directing payouts to revenue vs. a priority for "quality revenue," which indicates that gross margin should be included in the plan.

If gross margins are included in your plan, the marketing team must be tightly aligned with sales to make sure that changes in margin expectations and cost structures are quickly communicated to the sales team, to reduce the opportunity for the team to turn away business that current conditions would warrant taking.

Having responsibility for gross margins is another good reason to include finance in the professional-skills training curriculum for your sales team. Salespeople will respond if, in addition to being incentivized, they understand the importance of margins and believe that they can impact them.

For most businesses, bookings should not be a part of your incentive plan. Bookings are more fungible than revenues, so there is more potential for bookings to move in or out of a quarter (effecting payouts) at the end of plan periods. Your plan will already have a substantial portion of the incentive allocated to revenue, and given bookings are simply revenue that just hasn't yet shipped, this base is covered.

However, paying on bookings may make sense in some capital-equipment businesses, where the booking represents a significant milestone in a long cycle to recognize revenue.

Other issues to consider when developing the revenue component:

- **Acceleration**—As an incentive for salespeople to exceed their plans, it is common to have the payouts richer after 100 percent of the target has been achieved.

  Begin with a view of how much acceleration is required to get the attention and focus of the team. For example, you may want to provide an opportunity to double the incentive payout for achieving 150 percent.

  After getting comfortable with a description of the overall messaging, careful modeling is needed to arrive at an acceleration curve with the right balance of incentive with an acceptable cost.

  The major change we made to our plan was to only provide accelerated payouts if the salesperson had shown growth over recent quarters rather than for simply beating that quarter's target.

  Specifically, our plan paid at the target rate of up to 100 percent (as in our example), and then an accelerator was applied if the salesperson had shown growth over recent quarters.

  A simple way to implement this type of accelerator is to take the rolling average of growth for the previous three quarters and pay against that. Sustained growth is a sure sign that good things are happening with the customer and therefore something you're happy to pay for.

  It also provides a way for salespeople to smooth their earnings a bit. For example, if they have a down quarter in the midst of a growth trajectory, the growth accelerator will increase the payout for that quarter (though the average will drop for the following quarters).

Our team became big fans of using revenue growth as a way of providing accelerated payments because it effectively tied results to rewards. No growth, no acceleration.

Key Point: *If your business is characterized by sharp changes in the revenue patterns at the customer level, using revenue growth over previous quarters is an effective way to provide accelerated payments for exceeding the revenue target.*

Another strategy to deal with variability is to put a portion of the revenue incentive toward achieving an annual number rather than a quarterly number. Achieving an annual target will reduce the impact of short-term variability with the added benefit of aligning sales toward hitting the company's annual operating plan.

- **lCliffs and Caps**—A cliff is a low-end threshold below which the salesperson gets zero payout. The theory behind a cliff is that the salesperson should generate a certain level of effort (hence result) before being eligible for any incentive pay. Cliffs may make sense in a business with no repeat revenue, such as our earlier door-to-door example, but they don't make sense in major-account incentive plans.

  Major accounts usually have a substantial existing revenue run rate so a very low performance to target usually signals a collapse in the customer's business. In this case, not getting an incentive check simply discourages a salesperson and may create a retention issue.

  Caps represent a threshold on the top end of the plan. Almost all incentive consultants will recommend against caps, making the point that the occasional "plan buster" payout provides a considerable incentive to the rest of the team. This is why you see jackpot winners on roadside billboards, as gamblers are more likely to visit casinos paying out the biggest jackpots.

In a major-account environment, caps on the high end are okay for the same reason that cliffs on the low end are a bad idea, since blowing out revenue on the high side is almost always driven by an unforecastable increase in a customer's business rather than the performance of the sales team. A cap also builds in limits to your cost of sales. That said, a cap should still allow for reasonable plan leverage and should be no lower than, say, 150 percent of target.

If you do decide to implement a cap, make sure it accommodates any "home run" scenarios, plus a little, that your team could drive and that you would want to encourage and incentivize.

- **Global support**—Adequately covering a major account often requires more than one salesperson to support the same revenue stream. The most common example occurs when the customer's product-development team is in a different location than the manufacturing location.

The incentive plan needs to allow all salespeople providing significant support to a revenue stream to have that revenue included in their plan. The simple approach is to split the revenue between the salespeople covering the product development, booking, and billing locations.

More sophisticated schemes can be implemented to allow for the total revenue number to be included into each salesperson's plan, but they are outside the scope of this chapter.

Key Point: *The revenue component of your plan is the most important and complex plan element to design and administer. Getting this right requires careful thought given to the upside available (what gets the team focused) and patience in building plan-acceleration curves that model your business environment and that you can afford.*

Goals

In addition to the focus they bring, including goals in the plan encourages good management practice by driving managers and their salespeople to learn how to write good goals. Goals also provide an incentive for non-quantitative results, such as bringing on a new channel partner or for other financial priorities that didn't make the cut in your plan, such as design wins or gross margin.

If you do include goals as a plan element, you will need to provide training on how to write them and be patient with the quality for several quarters. Early on, the goals will be too easy, or goals will be suggested for activities that are clearly just a part of the job.

In addition to providing training, you can manage around these issues by personally approving all goals and only allowing them to be a small percentage of the incentive target—in the range of 10 to15 percent. This will require an upfront time commitment on your part, but it is a good investment to ensure quality and to develop your team's skills.

In terms of mechanics, a good approach is to allow the salesperson to suggest three to five goals with total weighting that adds up to 125 percent. The goal should be crafted so that good execution yields a payout at 100 percent and if they significantly exceed their goals they get a modest acceleration to the payout up to 125 percent. Defining "good execution" to 100 percent performance isn't easy, which is another reason why you should leave them as a minor portion of the incentive target.

Even with limited participation in the payout, goals can bring significant focus to your team for a limited investment. Setting aside 10 to15 percent of the incentive budget to develop a goal-oriented sales team is an excellent investment.

Key Point: *Including goals as a plan element creates a goal-driven organization and provides a way to include metrics that don't merit a dedicated plan element.*

Design Wins

Given that closing new business is the lifeblood of your company, design wins need to be included in the plan. They can be included as a specific plan element with mechanics based on performance to a target (like revenue), or they can be included in a bonus program. A third option is to include them in the goals portion of the plan.

A clear definition of what constitutes a design win is crucial to maintaining plan integrity. Production purchase orders or signed (billable) contracts are the best options. You also need to think through how to deal with the quality of the revenue for each win. Specifically, while all design wins are important, getting wins in new product categories is more difficult, and given these wins drive your growth, you may want to provide a richer incentive for them.

There are many issues that need to be agreed upfront, including which opportunities are eligible for an incentive, if payments will be available for partial wins or milestones, who makes these decisions, and many more. In summary, design wins need to be a part of your plan, but given the complications of not being a simple number, such as revenue, implementation needs to be thought through carefully.

Recognition Programs

There are a number of ways—both positive and negative—to provide incentives outside of the compensation plan. These programs are driven by the idea—an idea that I believe deeply—that salespeople are primarily motivated by recognition. Even money, at root, is a form of recognition.

On the positive side, the most effective approach is some sort of executive recognition, such as a President's or CEO's Club. These programs only work if the sponsoring executive takes this on personally and has an active hand in the design and personalization of the program.

There are many ways to do it, but it must be exclusive, so that participation sets the winners apart. If it can involve the salesperson's spouse, such as a vacation for all the winners with the CEO and his or her spouse, you'll increase the number of people generating pressure for results.

Our CEO and Founder at National Semiconductor, Charlie Sporck, had such a club, titled "Charlie's Club." Winners were treated to a vacation in Hawaii, capped by a dinner at Charlie's beachfront home on the north shore of Oahu. These were memorable experiences and big motivators to those few of us who earned the right to be members of the club.

As noted in the discussion regarding guiding principles, these types of programs only work if they're essentially the CEO's idea.

Data-based recognition programs can also motivate if done carefully and in a professional manner. An example of data-based recognition is publishing performance to plan for the entire sales team on a regular basis.

Key Point: *Recognition programs outside of the compensation plan can be powerful motivators, particularly those sponsored by the President/CEO.*

CONSTRUCTING THE PLAN

The first rule is that the plan should be simple, both in terms of the number of plan elements and the complexity of those elements. Fewer plan elements will increase the focus on those plan elements included.

Key Point: *The plan should be simple, with few plan elements and calculations that preferably can be done in the salesperson's head. Simple plans set clear priorities. Salespeople must find it easy to know exactly where they stand. When in doubt, leave it out.*

Figure 2 below outlines a sample plan that includes three elements: revenue, design wins, and a goal component.

Plan Element	Terms
Revenue	No Acceleration in payouts of up to 100% of Revenue Target.
	Payout at 150% for revenue over 100% of Revenue Target.
	Plan caps on the top end at 175%. No cliffs on the bottom end.
	85% of Incentive Target applied to Revenue Performance.
Goals	Direct Manager must approve eligible goals.
	Total Weighting of Goals to sum to 125% (maximum payout).
	15% of Incentive Target applied to Goal Performance.
New Business Win	Bonus applies only to Strategic Products (published list).
	$3000 bonus for each win.

Figure 8.2. Sample Plan with Terms and Payouts

The example plan aligns well with the guiding principles developed earlier. Revenue performance is the primary priority, yet design wins are considered important enough to drive a bonus on top of the incentive plan. Goal performance receives a modest payout and will provide some discretionary focus to be approved by the salesperson's manager. One of the goals must be a gross-margin target, so that the third guiding principle is included in the plan.

A different option that still aligns with our guiding principles would be to eliminate the plan element for goals and replace it with an element for design wins. Weighting for revenue could be dropped from 85 percent to 70 percent, creating substantial priority for design wins but not requiring an additional bonus payout.

There are a number of possibilities, but be sure to make the hard choices and keep the plan simple, including no more than three plan elements.

To demonstrate the calculations for the example in Figure 2, consider a salesperson with a total compensation package of $100K with a 70/30 split between base and incentive. In this case, performance to revenue targets would account for 85 percent of the $30K incentive ($25.5) and the balance would apply to performance to goals.

Figure 3 shows how the payouts would be calculated assuming 125 percent performance to target on revenue, 110 percent performance to goals, and one design win. The calculations are for one quarter of performance ($7500 total incentive at 100 percent).

Plan Element	Payout Calculation	
Revenue	Payout Available—$7500 X .85=$6375	
	Payout for 125% performance = $6375 for hitting target (up to 100%) + 25% of $6375 (for exceeding 100%) X 1.5	
	Calculation— $6375 + $2390 = **$8765**	
Goal Performance	Payout Available—$7500 X .15 = $1125	
	Payout for 110% 1.1 X $1125 = **$1238**	
New Business Win	One Approved Win --> **$3000**	
Totals	Revenue Component	**$8,765**
	Goal Performance Component	**$1,238**
	New Business Win Bonus	**$3,000**
	Incentive Payout Total	**$13,003**

Figure 8.3. Example Payouts for the Sample Incentive Plan in Figure 2

Shorter plan periods and hence more frequent payouts better align rewards with results, but this needs to be balanced against the resources needed to administer the payouts. Also consider how your company closes periods. Quarterly payouts are common in public companies given they close on quarter boundaries. This also strikes a reasonable balance between payout frequency and administrative costs.

When constructing your plan, make sure to involve sales management and the sales team in the process. It is your job to set the priorities and approve the plan, but your team cares a lot about the incentive plan, so you'll surely get thoughtful feedback if you include them. Involving your team will increase the odds that the plan will both meet your objectives and be well-received by the team.

ADMINISTERING THE PLAN

Plan Hygiene

Because incentive plans affect compensation, problems with the plan can cause serious morale issues or worse, cause the company to end up in court. The first defense is to have a well-documented plan. In addition to clearly stating terms, the plan should show examples of all calculations used to determine the payouts.

Be sure to have a disclaimer that makes clear that the plan can be changed at any time by the plan administrator (usually the VP Sales or CEO) and that any decisions made are final and binding. If you are forced to make a ruling on an incentive question, it's a sign that there is some ambiguity in your plan, so make sure to circle back and amend the plan to reflect the precedent set by your decision.

Making incentive payouts as soon as possible after the close of the incentive period will maximize motivation, but at least be sure to cut incentive checks when promised. Late checks are a huge negative.

Key Point: *Good hygiene, such as clear, well-documented plans and incentive checks paid on time, is expected. Any sloppiness around administration of the plan will be a de-motivator for your team.*

Managing During a Plan Period

Obviously, you'll generate the most positive energy around targets that your team believes they can beat. However, sometimes the market turns down after performance targets are set. In these cases, the team will be given difficult and perhaps nearly unreachable targets.

In these cases, you'll surely be asked by your team to reduce the targets. "No," is the answer to this question and make sure to say it quickly. It is, after all, why it is called "at risk" income. If you change targets once, the expectation is that they will be dropped in every downturn. The Lord giveth and the Lord taketh away, as the Good

Book says. For sure you won't be asked by your team to raise targets during an upturn. The only exception to this rule is the rare case where corporate targets are changed, in which case incentive targets should be changed to retain alignment.

Key Point: *Never make changes to the plan targets based on market conditions. It is the quickest path to destroying the credibility of your plan.*

Occasionally, there will be incentive cases that are not clearly covered by the plan that require a ruling. When making these decisions, keep two rules in mind: (1) the ruling should be consistent with the spirit of the plan, not what seems fair at the moment, and (2) be very concerned about the precedent set by your decision. A bad decision will come back time and again and become "the gift that keeps on giving."

If you run a large team and are therefore likely to get several issues needing resolution in a plan period, you may want to consider an incentive-review board. Conceptually, this is a court, with the "plaintiff" presenting their written case for relief. A review board composed of representatives from the sales team, sales management, HR, and finance, reviews the cases. After meeting to review the cases, the review board provides an opinion to the plan executive who then makes the final decision.

Evolving the Plan

As the sales executive, you will find it is good practice to review all payouts at the end of each plan period to determine if the company is getting a good return on its incentive-plan investment. Specifically, did those who got large payouts deserve them, and did the reasons for significant misses make sense?

When you encounter payouts you're not comfortable with, drill into the situation to understand why, as this may lead to changes in your plan. Reviewing payouts was what generated my concern for our plan, which led to the development of the growth accelerator discussed earlier.

Key Point: *It is good practice to review payouts after each plan period to make sure you're comfortable with them. If not, understand why and make sure to fold needed changes into next year's plan.*

SUMMARY

Your incentive plan will definitely impact your team's performance either positively or negatively. Designing and administering a great plan will require a substantial time commitment, but it is well worth it.

Before choosing from among the many options to include in your plan, you need to align with the other executives on the priorities for the coming year, and from that develop a set of guiding principles to keep the plan aligned as it develops.

At the end of each plan year, you should review the incentive payouts to confirm that payouts were consistent with the company's performance. That review, and consideration of any rulings that were made during the year, will inform whether you need to consider changes to the plan for the next year.

If your team is going to "break the bank" with your incentive plan (as you hope they do), they'll need to win the big, high-value deals. The next chapter will present a process for leading the team to those wins.

"You've got to know when to hold 'em, know when to fold 'em,
Know when to walk away, know when to run . . ."

Kenny Rogers, from "The Gambler"

(August 21, 1938–)

WINNING BIG DEALS

The primary role of sales is to find a "win-win" position for the company and customer, and then, to close both sides. For a salesperson negotiation is a way of life, from finding a fair and reasonable way to solve daily customer problems to concluding a significant contract negotiation.

Many of us have been in a negotiation with a lot of revenue riding on the outcome and the customer telling us that we'll lose the business unless we drop our prices much lower than we're prepared to go.

What to do?

In this situation, making the best decision regarding whether "to hold'em, or fold 'em," as Kenny Rogers says, is a matter of understanding the value of your position against the customer's other live options.

Developing that needed understanding is a matter of taking the time to prepare properly. As obvious as this sounds, the pressing concerns of the moment and the lack of a good method too often push the important task of preparation to the last second.

Each year there are a handful of high-value negotiations and new business opportunities within your major accounts where a good outcome is crucial to the health of your company.

It's the sales executive's responsibility to install processes and a culture around those methods that prepare your company to maximize results from important opportunities.

Key Point: *Improving processes that drive preparation for significant opportunities is the most significant way for a sales executive to impact gross margins.*

Processes that prepare your team for these must-win negotiations and opportunities are the focus of this chapter. For near-term revenue, we'll discuss how to get organized to win annual volume negotiations, and for design wins, we'll discuss implementation of Miller Heiman's Strategic Selling, the best-of-breed process for winning new business opportunities.

Job One is making sure that the current revenue stream is protected; so the first topic is preparing for negotiations around your current production business. This revenue can take many forms, from annual sales of components, supplies, services, or even recurring licenses.

Although the section below will use annual volume negotiations for a components business as a model, the preparation process can easily be generalized to any business.

RECURRING VOLUME NEGOTIATIONS

Negotiations for your current production business are usually scheduled on a recurring annual or semiannual basis. In these cases, current production volume is put up for rebid and the process culminates with suppliers receiving a share of the next period's business based on the results of the negotiation.

Objectives for annual volume negotiations should be included in each strategic account plan, a topic covered in the chapter on major-account planning. If the account plan has received executive approval, you'll be a step ahead as the organization will be aligned on the objectives for the negotiation before preparation begins.

Customers have their own pattern for preparing for negotiations, but it is common for each supplier to be given a package of information with the detail needed to make a bid, such as expected volumes and target selling prices for qualified products. The customer also sets a date for the negotiation.

Negotiation Calendar

Three milestones are relevant in the preparation for each negotiation: (1) development of the negotiating package by the sales and marketing team, (2) approval by the executive team, and (3) closing the negotiation. Your negotiation calendar should include dates for each of these milestones.

The biggest enemy of good preparation is starting too late, so ensure the milestone dates allow for adequate preparation and publish them as early in the season as possible. Leave a buffer of at least a week between the executive approval meeting and the negotiation. This extra time will often be needed to close any issues left unresolved at the approval meeting.

This calendar, along with folders to archive documents is an excellent application to integrate into your customer resource management (CRM) platform. If you're not on a CRM, Microsoft Outlook can be an acceptable option as well. You will likely need an administrative resource to maintain the calendar and send out milestone reminders, given the amount of work involved.

Key Point: *Creating and actively managing a calendar that includes the preparation milestones and negotiation dates for all of your major-account negotiations is more important than it might at first appear. A large number of milestones need to be tracked for each negotiation, and this is further complicated by the fact that many customers schedule these negotiations for the fourth calendar quarter, essentially creating a "contract season."*

All of those involved in the preparation or approval loop should have access to the calendar. With a calendar in place to drive the process, the next step is to build a data package based on a standard template, which will ensure both the quantity and quality of the information provided.

Milestone 1: Sales and Marketing Preparation Package

Preparation of the package starts with the information provided by the customer. At minimum this should include forecasted volumes and the customer's price targets.

Significant negotiations have many of the aspects of a battle situation. To begin, both sides don't have all of the information they need. Thus, the key initial objective is learning as much as possible about the positions of your customer and your management team, then navigating conflicts to an agreed settlement that works for both sides. Like a good battle plan, your negotiating strategy must have clear objectives, a considered opinion of the competition's positions and an understanding of your relative strengths (to leverage) and weaknesses (to minimize).

The account manager owns the account strategy and is therefore responsible to drive the process that generates the negotiating strategy. Marketing team members bring critical product-specific knowledge and responsibility for their own P&L to the discussion. Marketing must be very active in the process and take ownership of the strategies developed and the financial results for the product lines they represent.

Key Point: *As with any team process, it is important that roles are clearly defined. While it is true that the account manager has ownership of the strategy and preparation process, each marketing team member must take ownership for the preparation, strategies, and most importantly, for the results for their product line.*

The sales and marketing team works together to achieve the first milestone, that of building a negotiation package that they as a team are comfortable with. This milestone prepares them to achieve the second: gaining executive approval for the negotiation package.

Creating a standard template for the negotiation package is an important way for you to control the quality and consistency of your team's preparation. The template should be approved by the other members of the executive team so that it includes their view on what information is required for review in the approval meeting.

The negotiation package should include the following information:

- **Overview/Objectives** – The overview should open with the objectives for the negotiation, both yours and the customer's. It should also summarize last year's revenues and margins with this customer and include target revenues, margins, and corresponding market shares for the period under negotiation.

  The objectives presented in the overview section are the overall or corporate objectives for the negotiation, which are total revenue, margin and share totals compared with the current period. Include any strategic objectives that go beyond the top-line financials, such as share in new and strategic products.

  Indicate your place in the order of the negotiations as this validates where you fit in the supply chain and may affect your negotiating strategy. Less strategic, primarily price-oriented suppliers are usually brought in first to generate aggressive (often unrealistic) price targets that can be used against more strategic suppliers scheduled toward the end of the negotiations.

  Make clear any environmental changes that may drive the customer's objectives or the tone of the negotiation, such as changes to their organization or business conditions.

  The overview section should remain brief, no more than two or three slides.

- **Product-Line Strategies** – Each product line should have a separate section that presents their strategy. Each product-line analysis should begin with an overview slide, which includes the previous period's results (revenues/margins/shares) and the objectives for the period to be negotiated.

One or two slides should be prepared that provide a statement of the overall product-line strategy and specific strategies for large revenue line items. This is the right place to state revenue, share, and margin targets.

Remember, a good strategy leverages strength and minimizes weakness. Therefore, products that may require relatively large concessions to hold share or where the company has leadership should be highlighted.

Specific strategies for high volume or otherwise strategic products should naturally follow. For example, the product line may be willing to provide more significant price reductions in the back half of the year, when cost reductions kick in, provided the customer is willing to maintain share at higher prices in the early part of the year.

With the key product strategies documented, line item or "by-product" detail on volumes and prices can then be provided sorting the largest revenue opportunities to the top.

The example below assumes a business with many products or line items, such as a components or pharmaceuticals business.

	Current Year					Initial Position				
Product	Volume	Price	Total $'s	Margin %	Share	Volume	Price	Total $'s	Margin %	Share
Prod A	800	$ 155	$ 124,000	50%	40%	2000	$ 175	$ 350,000	65%	40%
Prod B	1500	$ 110	$ 165,000	46%	65%	2400	$ 125	$ 300,000	55%	65%
Prod C	6000	$ 100	$ 600,000	36%	50%	10000	$ 110	$1,100,000	70%	50%
Family Total	8300	$ 107.11	$ 889,000	40%	51%	14400	$ 121.53	$1,750,000	67%	51%

	Expected Result					Walkaway Position				
Product	Volume	Price	Total $'s	Margin %	Share	Volume	Price	Total $'s	Margin %	Share
Prod A	1500	$ 150	$ 225,000	51%	45%	1000	$ 140	$ 140,000	45%	40%
Prod B	1700	$ 100	$ 170,000	45%	65%	1200	$ 100	$ 120,000	40%	65%
Prod C	8000	$ 90	$ 720,000	37%	55%	6500	$ 85	$ 552,500	32%	50%
Family Total	11200	$ 99.55	$1,115,000	41%	55%	8700	$ 93.39	$ 812,500	36%	50%

Figure 9.1. Example of the Negotiation Package

Figure 1 presents an example of the product-specific detail that should be prepared for each product line as part of the strategy review. This example presents a reasonably healthy business, where the sales and marketing team expects to grow revenues and share while maintaining margins.

The current year results should be presented alongside the initial position, the expected result, and walk-away position. Laying out the information in this way presents the strategy in a logical progression by showing the team's initial position, where they think it will end, and a potential worst-case scenario that must be planned for.

To define terms, the *expected result* is the outcome the team believes they can close based on their current view of competition. The *walk-away position* provides the worst-case scenario the team believes they may face during the negotiation. If the customer isn't willing to settle for these terms, the team is willing to "walk away" from the opportunity.

Although one hopes not to run into these worst-case or potential "walk away" situations, it is important to have alignment up and down the organization to ensure the team is prepared and has the confidence to handle even the most difficult situation that may arise.

The negotiation package should be approved by all relevant sales and marketing management prior to review in the executive approval meeting.

Milestone 2: Executive Approval

The purpose of the executive approval meeting is to approve strategies and negotiating positions that will empower the sales and marketing team to negotiate with confidence.

Of course, preparing good strategies is the most important prerequisite to a successful executive review. Most negotiations will involve a few products where negotiating to an acceptable result will be difficult. Therefore, it is wise to publish the negotiating package early, allowing time for the executive team to review the material and for you to schedule pre-meetings with relevant executives with responsibility for products that may be difficult to negotiate.

Key Point: *There is always danger of not getting off the first page when presenting many numbers to a crowd of analytical executives. Working difficult issues before the meeting, combined with a well-thought through negotiation package provided before the review, will increase the odds for a productive executive review.*

After completing the review of each product line strategy, the discussion should turn toward strategies that leverage corporate strength to grow share. Examples include bundles across product lines, corporate level rebates, or service programs.

Key Point: *Don't let any of your sales team flunk their sales IQ test by proposing a bundle where gross margin dollars are sacrificed in one product line to take unacceptable business in another.*

You should also discuss any pre-positioning needed prior to the negotiation. It is usually better to alert the customer to any dramatic and unexpected positions you may take, rather than risk a surprise that derails the negotiation.

The issue of impasse or "deadlock" situations must be covered, and it is the responsibility of the executive team to make sure there are clear running rules to handle these. Ideally, someone at the negotiation is empowered to make any decisions not previously agreed during the executive review. Otherwise, someone designated by the executive team needs to be reachable by phone during the negotiation.

Key Point: *It is the executive's responsibility to clarify how deadlock or "walk away" decisions are to be handled. There is no better way to set the negotiating team up for failure than to send them into battle not knowing how the tough calls are to be made.*

Given the importance of the decisions made in this meeting, it is important to document the outcome, including any actions that still require closure.

Schedule these reviews for an hour. An hour is enough time to complete your objective, and the tight schedule will keep you focused. If more time is required, it is better to regroup and schedule a follow-on session, if needed, so that people are fresh. Scheduling the initial review at least a week before the negotiation will allow time for any required follow-on meetings.

Milestone 3: Closing the Negotiation

The topic of handling direct negotiations is a science unto itself supported by a large body of literature to which the reader is directed. This chapter will touch on just a few points that are important to consider when making your preparations.

Every customer has his or her own negotiating style. Some prefer to pre-negotiate as many line items as possible and leave only a few high-value products for a formal negotiating meeting while others prefer to start and complete the negotiation in one session. These factors obviously affect the attendees from your side and who plays which role in the negotiation. The customer sets the rules. Your role is to make sure your team is organized and best prepared to play by them.

For the formal negotiation, the account manager attends, as well as a point person from marketing for each product line or group of product lines. As with all negotiations, the more people involved, the harder it is to control the meeting, so it is generally good to keep attendees to only those required to drive the discussion and make decisions. A pre-meeting with the negotiating team should be held the night before to drive alignment.

Key Point: *The account manager should hold a pre-meeting just prior to the negotiation to provide late-breaking news, review roles and ground rules. An effective pre-meeting will ground the team and ensure they are aligned for the negotiation.*

The account manager leads this meeting by providing real-time updates, reviewing the objectives, negotiating positions, and outlining how the negotiation is expected to flow. It is important to ensure that everyone understands his or her role for the negotiation, specifically who will lead which sections and how to call for breaks.

As mentioned earlier, the account team is responsible to organize the various product-line strategies in a way that can be presented as a coherent corporate strategy to the customer. If possible, you should lead off the negotiation by presenting a brief description of the company's strategy and relevant information, such as investments in strategic product categories, service guarantees, and market shares, which demonstrate your corporate strength.

While the account manager leads the meeting and drives the pace, each marketing team member should drive the discussion for their product portfolio and make specific decisions for their products since they are responsible for their product line P&L's.

The customer will likely dictate the flow and order of the negotiation, but to the extent possible, get the products most important to you to the front of the discussion when you have maximum flexibility and people are fresh.

After the negotiation is complete, it is the account manager's responsibility to make sure the results and any action items are documented both to the customer and to the marketing teams.

Key Point: *Effectively managing the real-time ebb and flow of a negotiation is a hallmark of your best account managers. Calling breaks and recalibrating the team when the team gets misaligned, or is about to make a mistake, demonstrates real leadership. In any case, make sure the team member assigned to lead the negotiation brings these skills to the negotiation.*

Successful annual volume negotiations are critical to maintaining your current revenue stream, but winning those few high potential new business opportunities is also a must to drive the trajectory of next year's business.

CLOSING HIGH VALUE NEW BUSINESS

The earlier chapters titled "Closing New Business" and "Account Planning" presented processes to track and drive new business opportunities to closure.

It stands to reason that any tool that increases the odds of winning these opportunities by even a few percent is well worth the investment. Strategic Selling from the Miller Heiman Company is such a tool.

This author has no formal affiliation with Miller Heiman but has become a big fan of the process based on personal experience using it to build more effective teams and better strategies for important new business opportunities. As you train and embed this process into your sales culture, you'll build selling skills and, in the process get a read on the current sales IQ of each member of your team.

Key Point: *Developing strategies through the Strategic Selling process will increase your closure rate. Driving Strategic Selling into your sales culture is the sales executive's single highest leverage activity to closing new business.*

In this section, I'll provide a very brief overview of the process and how to roll it out in your organization.

Strategic Selling Overview

The objective of Strategic Selling is to build a winning strategy for complex opportunities in an environment characterized by constant change. In this context, the term *complex* refers to the presence of multiple customer-stakeholders in the decision process; each needing different results from your solution.

For example, those who design a product will have different concerns than those who manufacture it. Strategic Selling organizes all of the relevant results for each of these stakeholders in one place and then brings your team together through a repeatable process to develop the best strategy for that moment in time.

Another important concept relates to how customers' needs are defined. Our instinct is to build our proposals solely to satisfy a customer's stated business results, such as meeting the requested product specifications, price, and delivery targets, etc.

We tend not to consider the personal side of stakeholder decisions. One of the powerful truths that Strategic Selling drives into your strategy is that a stakeholder only advocates for your solution when you satisfy BOTH business results and their personal interests.

In addition to building these business results into the strategy, Strategic Selling also takes the important, but usually forgotten step of mapping out these personal interests of each stakeholder and folding actions that address those needs into the strategy.

The process also has a heavy focus on developing coaches, i.e., key people positioned with your customer to provide critical information at crucial times. Coaching makes the difference early and late in the selling process. Strategic Selling provides an early and constant focus on building these coaching relationships so they are available when needed.

All of the relevant information comes together in a one-page strategy document during a 60-minute, team-based review meeting.

The team-oriented nature of Strategic Selling is one of its strengths. Strategy reviews provide the opportunity for account managers to work collaboratively with marketing and sales management to develop strategy and to align on actions.

To learn more about Strategic Selling beyond this brief introduction, contact Miller Heiman at www.millerheiman.com.

Key Point: *Holding an effective strategy review will increase your odds of winning but it does represent a significant investment of your team's time, so limit its use to those few "must win" opportunities.*

Developing a Strategic Selling Culture

Training your team in the Strategic Selling process can be accomplished in a number of weeks, but making the process a part of your selling culture requires a long-term commitment from you, the sales executive.

Training your team is only the first step of the process, something you can arrange with the Miller Heiman team. Coming out of the training, the energy level will be high as your team sees the potential of the process. After the initial euphoria, you will encounter inertia as the team struggles to develop new skills and make them part of their daily routine.

There are a number of actions you can take to make the Strategic Selling process a habit, the way your team naturally builds strategy.

First, you must make clear that Strategic Selling is not a "program of the month," that it is not going away.

Be sure to agree on the initial set of opportunities that will be managed under this process and maintain a formal calendar for the strategy reviews. Embedding the process into the calendar sends a strong signal that the process is here to stay.

Your administrator should manage the calendar, but each account manager must own his or her reviews. For each review, the account manager needs to determine which team members to invite and then ensure that the one page review form is completed and distributed to all attendees prior to the review.

Early in the adoption of the process, these reviews will tend to capture the usual tactical actions, but will be weak precisely in the areas you are trying to improve, such as developing coaches or in developing plans to meet the customer stakeholder that holds the purse strings (usually one of the customer's senior executives).

Your initial instinct will be to participate in as many reviews as possible and lead by example. However, having the most senior sales executive in attendance will make some attendees self-conscious and will detract from the free-form, brainstorming feel that these meetings need.

To get expertise into the reviews without the distraction of the sales executive attending, designate a few key members of the sales team who have demonstrated skill with the process as Strategic Selling champions. These champions should be assigned to participate in and coach strategy reviews.

Key Point: *Designating Strategic Selling Champions is an effective way to improve strategies and the team's strategy development skills. It is also an opportunity to provide recognition to the best members of your sales team.*

In addition to bringing needed expertise to the reviews, designating champions provides an opportunity to recognize your best salespeople and reinforce the importance of the program to the rest of the organization.

You should hold a monthly call with these champions to gauge progress and get their input on ways to better drive the process into your sales culture. It's a great way to bypass layers of management in your organization and improve your view of what is going on at the ground level.

Training your team is easy, but changing culture is hard. That is why many companies waste so much money on training that never sticks. As with all good things, patience and commitment are required. If you make that investment and develop a Strategic Selling organization, it will be a real differentiator for your organization.

SUMMARY

Like any good manager, you want to make sure you are spending your time on the things with the most leverage to drive your business.

Winning high-potential volume negotiations and design wins require different processes, but they both benefit from early, structured preparation.

Successful implementation of these processes will drive positive change in your sales culture. Be prepared for a long, slow journey that will require significant commitment and patience on your part. It is the essence of leadership to have a clear goal and the patience and drive to make it happen.

The next and last chapter will pull all of the processes together into a single management system. Just as the juggler keeps all of those plates spinning at one time, the sales executive needs to manage the team in a way that provides visibility and alignment with a reasonable time commitment by your team. After all, they can only sell if they are in front of the customer.

"What you do not measure, you cannot control."

Tom Peters

(November 7, 1942–)

WALKING THE TIGHTROPE

The idea behind Tom Peters' quotation goes all the way back to Lord Kelvin. The Enlightenment project itself was grounded in the idea that what you don't measure, you can't understand.

This is certainly true in business today.

As a sales executive, you walk a tightrope. Fall to one side and you spend all your time managing the numbers and neglecting the real priority: your customers. You can be sure that while you're in your office looking at numbers or sitting in a meeting, the competition is in front of your customers building their business and maybe taking some of yours.

But fall to the other side and you become disconnected with your team, losing your grip on their priorities and progress, or lack of it. You lose the ability to accurately forecast and are reduced to hoping that key opportunities are on track to closure. The result is surprise on the downside, and surprise usually points to a lack of control.

Key Point: *The surest sign of a mature sales executive is the ability to strike the right balance between making a personal impact in closing deals while staying in control of the business.*

The only way to strike this balance is to maintain a coordinated set of review processes structured to appropriately balance the team's focus. This allows you to provide leadership on strategy and to ensure that the team is on track to meet its commitments.

Objective	Examples	Frequency
Tactical Management	Staff Meetings, Revenue Reviews, Account Reviews, Design-Win Reviews	Weekly/Monthly
Long-Range Development	Goal Development Meetings, Staff Off-Site Meetings, Corporate Sales Meetings	Quarterly/Annual

Figure 10.1. Major Account Management Framework

Figure 1 provides a hierarchy of reviews and planning meetings that drive strategy and provide regular opportunities to measure progress and "course correct" as needed.

At first glance, Figure 1 seems to suggest a lot of meetings, and we all hate meetings, right? What we should hate is meetings without clear objectives and outcomes. The problem is almost always a lack of preparation and discipline, that is, sloppiness. Properly conceived and led, meetings can be a highly leveraged part of your team's busy day. To Tom Peters' point, reviews are the opportunity for us to measure so we can remain in control.

Key Point: *Regularly scheduled reviews that efficiently work through predefined objectives are the most efficient way to stay on track to your goals.*

An effective goal-development process is the core of any effective sales-management program, so we will lead with that topic first.

The discussion then moves to the limited, but effective, use of staff meetings and reviews to "track and drive" progress to your goals. Reviews can be a very efficient use of your time provided there is good follow-up. This requires that a skilled administrative resource be allocated to keep the calendar and any assigned action items straight.

With a framework in place to manage the current quarter business, we'll close the chapter by discussing effective implementation of planning meetings that are more strategic, such as staff off-site meetings and corporate sales meetings.

GOALS

Effective goal processes can only flourish in a culture that welcomes the opportunity to set stretch goals and regularly measure progress to their achievement. The positive side of a missed goal is the opportunity to learn.

To foster this kind of culture, missed goals cannot be used as clubs. When they are, goals are then seen as something to be gamed and managed, rather than as a way to focus, stretch, and learn. Of course, if a missed goal is part of a pattern of poor execution, the reasons for poor execution need to be addressed but not as part of how you develop and use goals with the team.

Scope of the Goal Process

An effective goal process drives a manager to align with each team member on key results that must be accomplished in the period under plan. Goals can be developed for any period of time, but a three-month quarter provides a good balance between the overhead of managing them and market visibility.

Goal development starts by asking the question, "What are those few things that need to be accomplished to allow me to look back at the end of the quarter and consider it a success?"

"Those few things" means as few as one and no more than five goals, so that the goals with milestones can fit on a single sheet of paper. By keeping goals to the few and important, each team member will be able to share their goals from memory.

Key Point: *To be effective, goals need to be written, both to improve clarity and to create a record. They also need to be completed early in the goal period so that they can be scored effectively when the period closes.*

The idea, then, is to have a few clearly written goals that a salesperson can carry on a sheet of paper. Scale that across your team, with everyone aligned on the results they need for a successful quarter, and you have a powerfully focused organization. As a bonus, scored goals are the best documentation of achievement (or lack of it) when it comes time to write annual employee reviews.

SMART Goals

The SMART criteria are tried and true tools for confirming that a goal is well-written. For a goal to be both clear enough to understand and that it can be scored properly at the end of the period, it must be:

- **Specific.** The goal needs to be clear enough that any two persons who read it will come away with the same understanding.

- **Measurable.** A hard-numeric metric is ideal. For example, when a goal states an increase in sales of a particular product, call out the size and timing of the increase. When the target is something qualitative, such as a better relationship with a customer, the goal needs to state specific milestones that can be documented, such as which executives should meet and what should be accomplished.

- **Achievable.** The goal must be realistically within the constraints of a solid effort and available resources. To include a goal whose final completion is outside the goal period, pick discrete milestones within that goal that are achievable within the period.

  For example, the final decision to award a design win may be outside the goal period but an important milestone, such as the commitment to complete a product evaluation may be achievable. This milestone makes an excellent goal for the current goal period.

  Take into consideration a particular team member's

propensity to under or overcommit. A team member is most committed when they believe their goals are achievable with some opportunity to beat them on the upside.

- **Relevant.** The relevant list of goals are those which, when looking back at the end of the quarter, answer our question, "Did we have a successful goal period?"

- **Time Based.** Include a target date for completion. Target dates should be on the liberal side of reasonable, since closing commitments usually take longer than expected. This helps team members develop the habit of hitting their goals.

  Prior to the start of a quarter, the goal process starts by building goals for the organization (i.e., your goals) using the model just discussed. These goals should tie to the corporate goals. Having these in place will allow you to "cascade" corporate goals through you to all levels of your organization. Said another way, goal results rolled up from the bottom should tie to the corporate goals.

With your goals in place, schedule a meeting with each team member to score goals from the previous quarter and discuss goals for the coming quarter. As preparation for the meeting, ask them to bring a rough list of potential achievements for the coming quarter that would answer our question, "What would make this a successful quarter?"

During that meeting, work the list to no more than five goals with associated milestones for each. Each goal may have up to four milestones that lead to that goal being realized. Also, assign weights to each goal that sum to 100 percent. Weighting clarifies priority and facilitates scoring. The meeting finishes with a draft-set of goals that your team member takes away to complete, including cross-checking them against the SMART criteria.

Key Point: *Goals need to be approved and in place before the end of the first week of the goal period at the latest, so schedule the initial meetings accordingly, leaving enough time for final approval and sign off.*

Starting too late is the second great sin of goal setting (the first is not following the SMART criteria). If you're chronically late approving goals, the whole process becomes an exercise in shooting first and calling whatever you hit the target.

Scheduling needs to include enough time to allow you to cascade goals through your team. The sales executive's goals should be completed before meeting with direct reports to ensure that the sum of the team's results achieve the group's (sales executive's) goals. And so it goes down the levels of the sales organization.

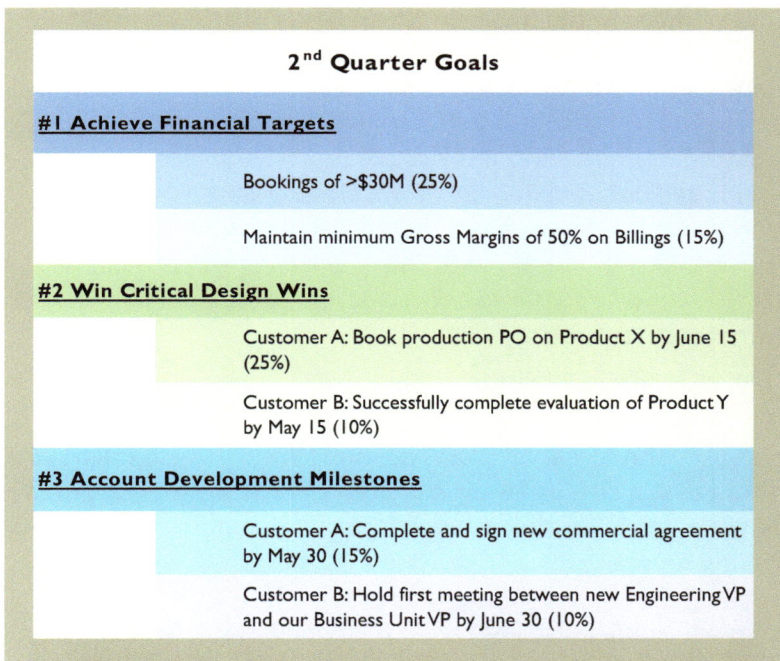

2nd Quarter Goals

2nd Quarter Goals

#1 Achieve Financial Targets

Bookings of >$30M (25%)

Maintain minimum Gross Margins of 50% on Billings (15%)

#2 Win Critical Design Wins

Customer A: Book production PO on Product X by June 15 (25%)

Customer B: Successfully complete evaluation of Product Y by May 15 (10%)

#3 Account Development Milestones

Customer A: Complete and sign new commercial agreement by May 30 (15%)

Customer B: Hold first meeting between new Engineering VP and our Business Unit VP by June 30 (10%)

Figure 10.2. Example Objective Set for a Salesperson

Figure 2 above shows an example of two goals that meet the SMART criteria. Based on the weightings in Figure 2, the most important results for this salesperson are to hit his or her bookings target and to close the design win with Customer A.

There are a number of ways to check progress to goals as you move through the goal period. Goals are an excellent agenda item if you have regular meetings with each of your staff. Or, team members could be tasked to forward the goals to you monthly with comments on progress.

Lastly, goals can be an agenda item during monthly account reviews. The point is that there are many low impact ways to ensure that goals become a regular part of your review process.

MANAGING THE QUARTER

As you move through the quarter, you need regular opportunities to review your progress on revenue and design-win targets and ensure you're closing opportunities and reacting quickly to problems.

Key Point: *Effective review meetings are "horizontal," moving quickly across items and only pausing for clarification or for discussion of an issue. Issues that can't be resolved quickly become "vertical"; that is, requiring extended discussion with only a few meeting participants. These items should be captured as actions for later discussion with only the required team members.*

Staff Meetings

Or should I say the "dreaded" staff meeting? While it's true that we've all sat through our share of long, meandering, and ultimately pointless staff meetings, it's a fact that the only thing worse than staff meetings is not having them at all.

Your team will come away energized if, in one hour or less, the team aligns on any quarter-close issues, gets an update on corporate news, and perhaps works through a topic together as a team. To make this happen, pick a regular time to meet, prepare, and then force yourself to keep the meeting to no more than an hour.

If possible, hold your staff meeting early in the week as a way to provide focus to the team as they launch their week. An agenda will require you to think through the objective and flow of the meeting and is helpful in managing the clock. A good agenda will include some subset of the following topics:

1. **Actions from the previous meeting.** Reviewing actions encourages compliance and provides context for the current meeting.
2. **Progress to revenue and design-win targets.** Staff meeting is not the place for a detailed review but, rather the forum to highlight overall progress and any significant disconnects from plan. Of course, in a revenue crisis, the recovery plan is THE topic for staff meeting.
3. **Corporate news.** Staff meeting is an efficient way to disseminate items of general interest, ranging from results of board meetings to changes in insurance coverage.
4. **Project discussion.** If time permits, you may want to schedule one or two topics that could be covered in-depth and require the team's input. Also, staff meeting is an efficient way for a product line or corporate function to work an issue with sales management.
5. **Review action items.** These are published to the team following staff meeting.

If you keep a brisk pace and through a clear agenda, your staff meetings will be a leveraged, efficient way to keep the team focused and to build team fabric.

Key Point: *Staff meetings, with few exceptions should be kept to an hour or less. It is your meeting and your responsibility to keep the discussion on track. In almost all cases, long staff meetings are a result of poor preparation and time management.*

Revenue-Review Meeting

As you move through the quarter, Job #1 is to make sure you maintain a solid grip on revenue for the quarter. An excellent revenue-management process was presented in the chapter titled "Driving the

Quarter." The weekly revenue review meeting is the axle around which that particular wheel spins.

The goal of this meeting is to build a clear picture, agreed between sales, marketing, and operations, of the high confidence revenue number at that moment in time and to identify actions to close gaps. My preference is to hold this meeting either at the beginning or the end of the week, since either schedule allows you to begin the week with a clear view of that quarter's revenue.

Holding staff meeting right after the revenue-review meeting is a perfect segue as you can then close the discussion on revenue before moving on to other topics.

Design Win and Account Reviews
While driving revenue for the quarter is the top priority, hitting the design-win target comes right behind in terms of importance. The chapter titled "Closing New Business" outlines how to hold an effective design-win review meeting.

The design-win review and revenue-review meetings have the same objective and similar formats. Specifically, it is cross functional, provides focus on high-value opportunities, and is action oriented.

The objective for an account review is to provide a platform for a salesperson to present progress to his or her numbers (revenue and design wins) along with his or her biggest obstacles to overcome and the resources required to reach these targets.

The decision regarding whether both account and design-win reviews are needed is largely a question of who needs to attend. The sales team is the execution arm of marketing, so if the marketing team wants access to the sales team to review design-win opportunities, both reviews may be required. Otherwise, design wins can be handled as part of an account review.

Given the dynamic nature of current-quarter revenue, the revenue-review meeting should be held weekly or biweekly. You likely can keep a good grip on the status of design wins and individual major accounts with a monthly review.

To maximize the precious time your team has to spend in front of customers, your team must not be required to do simple data gathering for these reviews. Rather, salespeople should only be required to organize their messaging to management into a slide or two and all other data should come directly from your information systems.

For example, data for design reviews should come directly from your CRM tool (e.g., Salesforce.com) and numbers for account reviews should simply be canned reports from the financial system.

Key Point: *To keep preparation time to an absolute minimum, all data to be reviewed for revenue and design wins should be reports available at the push of a button.*

Start the review by recapping results from the period under review and the status of actions taken from the last meeting. The last slide should be a free-form slide that allows the salesperson to articulate what he or she needs to hit his or her goals, what management needs to improve to make the company more competitive, and any useful competitive information.

With this minimalist approach, a salesperson can be reviewed in thirty to forty minutes. Keeping a short leash on these meetings keeps preparation to a minimum and forces the discussion to key messages. If problems are uncovered that require deeper discussion, an action item should be taken for later follow up. It's remarkable what you can learn and the energy that can be generated from a crisp set of reviews.

For many organizations, Friday is a good day for reviews, as they tend to be less demanding in terms of other scheduled meetings and travel.

Your follow-up on issues raised by your team is important to the credibility of any review. The sales team will support these reviews if they feel they are given an opportunity to be heard, the information is then used to drive change, AND there is minimal administrative burden.

Review Meeting	Frequency	Objective
Staff Meeting	Weekly	Review Actions
		Progress to Quarter Targets
		Corporate News
		Project Discussion
Revenue Review	Weekly	Validate Revenue Position
	Biweekly	Actions to Close Gaps
Design Win Review	Monthly	Validate Design Win Strategies
		Review Actions to Close Wins
Account Reviews	Monthly	Provide Market Status to Mgt
		Status Progress to Targets
		Validate Design Win Strategies
		Review Progress to goals

Figure 10.3. Summary of Review Meetings with Frequency and Objectives

A review of Figure 3 highlights that with two one-hour meetings (staff meeting and revenue review), your team can be updated and aligned for the upcoming week. In addition, you have a good grip on the revenue picture and the actions needed to close to target. This is a very leveraged use of your time.

You have the rest of the month and quarter to schedule the other reviews, and you can organize these in a fashion that best works for you.

PLANNING AND DEVELOPMENT MEETINGS

The life of the sales executive seems like a constant drive to hit the current-quarter revenue and design-win targets, then when the quarter is over . . . repeat.

To evolve your program and strategy, you must set aside time regularly to plan. Staff "off-site" and corporate sales meetings are tools to set your strategic agenda, drive alignment across the organization, and inject new energy into the team.

Staff Off-Site Meetings

Important but not urgent topics, such as incentive planning, preparing for the upcoming negotiation season, or extending core processes like your CRM are important topics that can be pushed to the side amidst the noise of driving the quarter.

An off-site staff meeting is just the place to work through these projects and allow your staff to build their leadership skills by taking the lead in preparing a topic and leading the team through it.

In addition to the opportunity to get away from the business and let the creative juices flow, these meetings are excellent team-building opportunities. The best place to build a personal relationship with a customer is out of their building at a restaurant or golf course, and this is also true with your team as well.

If travel is required for your staff, you can rotate locations so members of your staff can also share the opportunity of hosting the team.

Avoid holding these meetings at corporate locations. The battle to keep phones turned off and the team focused is almost not winnable unless you're off-site. This will provide needed physical and emotional separation from the business.

A successful off-site requires significant planning. Building the agenda and assigning time slots is the easy part. Each topic should have its own slide deck that opens with a list of objectives for that section. For that section, think carefully through how the discussion will progress and document the key points and issues that need discussion.

Finally, the deck should end with a specific list of deliverables, whether they are decisions required or assignments for follow-up later. As each section ends, the results for each deliverable, along with any action items, should be documented for publication after the meeting.

In terms of frequency, more than once a quarter is too often and fewer than once a year is probably not enough.

Corporate Sales Meetings

There is no better way to train and drive alignment between executive management and their sales team than to hold a worldwide sales meeting. It's also a great way to pump up your team. Hold a great sales meeting and expect a spike in bookings.

Sales meetings should have some mix of these objectives: (1) align the sales team to the corporate objectives and plan, (2) product training, and (3) generating energy and momentum.

Discussions around a potential sales meeting should start directly with your CEO since a corporate sales meeting is the CEO's meeting. You should outline your suggested objectives and calendaring and meeting length, provide a rough idea of cost, and—given these things are always very expensive—why you believe the timing is right to hold a meeting.

After gaining CEO approval, and after getting input from your peers on the executive team, planning can begin in earnest. If the meeting will have fewer than 25 attendees, you can handle the planning with help from one good administrator.

As the number grows, you'll need to resource accordingly. For example, if you're planning for a meeting with more than 100 attendees, you'll need to chair a team to plan the logistics and another to oversee creation of the training materials.

A larger meeting will take at least a quarter to build all the training and to obtain reasonable prices on venues. With the date set, you start with a kickoff with each planning team and then meet at least weekly thereafter to make sure preparations stay on track.

The presentation agenda should provide a mix of corporate plan review and product training. All of your corporate executives should be in attendance and present the plans for their businesses. Done right, these presentations will generate positive energy, so it often works well to start and end the day with an executive presentation.

Product training as a rule should be prepared and presented by the marketing teams. Whereas executives can be given a lot of flexibility in their presentations, the format for product training should be quite rigid.

The quality of marketing teams tends to be uneven in most companies and a specific, almost "fill in the blanks" template will reduce the number of editing loops required after your initial review. A consistent approach will also aid in retention, as the sales team will know what to expect as they move through the training.

In addition to presenting product-line strategy and the features/benefits of focus products, each presentation should have a clear call to action. The best presentations will also include selling tools such as cross-reference guides and summaries or "cheat sheets," which your teams can (and will) use when they return to the field.

If your team is selling technical products you may also need presentations on how your products fit into your customer's business so your team can speak more knowledgeably with customers and build a more consultative-type relationship.

Outside speakers can be used to spice up the agenda and are often a good way to close a day. Industry pundits or motivational speakers can work well, but it is even better to have a few customer executives present.

Customers are surprisingly willing to participate as they get an opportunity to present their company story and tell a major supplier what to improve in order to serve them better. It's also a great opportunity to build a relationship with a key customer executive.

As a meeting stretches toward a weeklong event, time should be set aside for a team building activity that combines some fun in the local area.

A great way to cap your sales meeting is with an awards dinner held on the final evening. Great care should be taken in choosing the recipients and types of awards, as there is an equal opportunity to end the meeting on a high or low note depending on how this is handled.

It is best to avoid "Salesperson of the Year" awards in favor of rewarding behaviors that you want reinforced in your culture. For example, you can give awards for "Going the extra mile to close an order" or "Going the extra mile to solve a customer problem."

Narratives are powerful ways of communicating values. When presenting awards, the story driving the award can be told with humor while emphasizing the values to be reinforced. You can give as many of these awards as time allows. It's a sure way to close your meeting with a bang.

SUMMARY

Every tightrope walker makes his or her way across the wire in his or her own style, so consider the range of review processes presented in this chapter as a menu of options from which you can choose to give you the type and level of control you need over your business.

Many management processes helpful to my career have been presented over the span of these chapters. Of course, they're really only useful if you, as the sales executive, develop a way to integrate them into your routine.

ABOUT THE AUTHOR

Scott Parker has over 25 years in the management of high technology companies in positions ranging from sales manager to CEO. The focus of his career has been on building revenue and high performing sales teams.

Scott is the father of four and resides in Mountain View, Ca

www.ingramcontent.com/pod-product-compliance
Lightning Source LLC
Chambersburg PA
CBHW041309210326
41599CB00003B/35